The Book of Modern Mountaineering

The Book of

Modern Mountaineering

Edited by
Malcolm Milne

with a Foreword by
the Rt Hon. the Lord Hunt of Llanvair Waterdine

G. P. Putnam's Sons
New York

I am deeply indebted to T. S. Blakeney for his help in compiling *The Book of Modern Mountaineering*. He advised on the original plan, read the contributions in manuscript and in proof and afforded me great assistance in securing photographs and in tracing elusive mountaineer-authors with a propensity for disappearing into the high hills. He declined to be named as co-editor but in fact performed most of the functions of that office. Without his encyclopaedic knowledge of the sport behind me, and his generous help at all stages, I could not have undertaken this editorship.

M.M.

Library of Congress Catalog Card Number 68-22544
Printed in Great Britain by Fleming & Humphreys (Baylis) Limited, Leicester

Contents

Foreword

by the Rt Hon. the Lord Hunt of Llanvair Waterdine

As I write this foreword the bookshelves beside me are heavy with the records of past adventures on the steep places of the earth, reaching back to the beginnings of this mysterious pastime called mountaineering. This book will shortly be joining the company of Mummery, Freshfield, Leslie Stephens and Guido Rey of the last century; and Buhl, Harrer, Gervasutti, Rébuffat and Bonington of modern times – and a host of others in between. *The Ascent of Everest* is there too in thirty different languages. There is, indeed, a mountain of literature on climbing.

I do not know what prompted each of these authors to publish their memories of exploration in remote ranges, or their struggles in the vertical on smaller mountains nearer home. But having felt the urge myself, I can guess what it was, and was not. For one thing, I believe that no true mountaineers have done so only, or even mainly, for financial gain as an end in itself: for some, of course, the gain was a means of setting out for the mountains once more. Nor do I believe that many have written in order to impress their prowess on the world at large, for climbing is a humbling experience – it makes you feel small. Most have found, in writing, a way of re-living experiences so vital to them that they have felt the need to prolong, or perpetuate them.

A few, I think, have written because they have a message for others who, without being mountaineers, can share the adventure with them; or better still, for those who may be inspired to go and discover it for themselves. This motive is perhaps the most important and it will be well achieved in this book.

The title relates to the present and points to the future but the material also draws upon the past. It is, indeed, a wide-ranging panorama of the whole mountain scene through the eye and memories of men of different generations and with different experience. The fact is that the modern tyro, with his amazing skill, stamina and daring, is a product of the deeds of those who have gone before him; his craft must be viewed against the background of the past. I am particularly glad that *The Book of Modern Mountaineering* has this perspective.

I am glad, too, to join with many old friends in the composition of this book. I know them nearly all and I have climbed with several of them. It is good to be re-united, whether it be on a mountain or in the printed word.

Henley-on-Thames — JOHN HUNT

Introduction

In gathering the material for this anthology my object has been to create, by means of a combination of text and photograph, as vivid an impression as possible of the modern mountain scene. The theme is one of contemporary knowledge and achievement set against a single chapter on the history of mountaineering. Ascents or exploration carried out prior to the 1939–45 War have only been mentioned to give, where necessary, a truer perspective.

Plainly a book of this sort must be highly selective: there are, as indeed there must be, notable omissions. The Andes, other than the Patagonian Andes and a photographic reference to Alpamayo, have received less coverage than such a magnificent range would warrant; the Southern Alps of New Zealand, the Caucasus and the North American Rockies have had but scant mention and as for the Nurseries . . . there are a hundred districts all with good claims to be included. And of course the company of mountaineers of international repute is a far larger one than is apparent from these pages.

Sad as it is to be so ruthlessly selective in a sport so rich in material I count myself more than fortunate in one essential particular . . . namely that of contributors. All are experts in their respective fields. I believe that their writings convey as authorative and accurate an impression of the contemporary sport as can be obtained and that they demonstrate, in conjunction with their pictures, that the modern mountaineer more than maintains the traditions of sensibility and erudition associated with the sport from the earliest days.

You, good reader, will be the judge. I can but ask that you judge this volume not as a comprehensive review but as an anthology which seeks to capture the essence of a noble sport: the essence not only of its techniques and achievements but something also of its philosophy and mysticism.

M.M.

Chapter 1

The Height of Achievement

For many, mountain achievement is a private contest between the mountaineer and the mountain, not to be measured by any universal rule. In this chapter, however, are described a number of recent, really major mountain triumphs which surely must be considered great by any measure

RECONNAISSANCE 1951 *W.H.Murray*

Mount Everest seemed to shrink back, utterly remote behind barriers of Asiatic mountain and desert, when China seized Tibet in 1950. The traditional but long approach to the north side was closed, at the least for a generation, while any approach through Nepal to the south side – always hitherto forbidden ground – would surely be more firmly barred than ever. That Everest might be climbed within three years was not a thought entertained by any sane mountaineer.

The event that flushed our nearly dead hopes was the trek into Sola Khumbu by Oscar Houston's American party in November 1950. H.W.Tilman, who had been refused entry only the year before, was now able to join them. On his return to London he read a paper to the Alpine Club, which the *Alpine Journal* printed in May 1951 together with his photograph of Everest's western icefall. This event had a most stimulating effect on Dr Michael Ward, Tom Bourdillon, and me, and in May we hopefully formed an Everest party to go out in the autumn – supposing that the Himalayan Committee would sponsor us and that the government of Nepal would assent.

Tilman seemed as pessimistic about the chance of finding a route as Mallory had been thirty years earlier, and so were all who knew Everest best. They had cause. In 1921, Mallory had climbed to the north-east col of Pumori from Tibet. He brought back a photograph showing an icefall plunging two thousand feet between the high west ridges of Everest and Nuptse. It showed nothing of the south col or the west cwm. The

Opposite: Ama Dablam stands over the approach.

Panorama from the west: North Peak, North Col, Everest (with the crest of the West Ridge plainly visible above the layer of stratus), Lhotse and, right, Nuptse.

top of the icefall at around 20,000 ft appeared to be flowing level from the invisible basin. If this were so, the south col slopes, four miles back, would rise 6,000 ft (the height of the Matterhorn above the Schwarzsee) in maybe half that distance.

Mallory's comment on the icefall was: 'We are not sorry we have not got to go up it. It is terribly steep and broken . . . It was not a very likely chance that the gap between Everest and the south peak could be reached from the west. From what we have seen now I do not much fancy it would be possible, even could one get up the glacier.' Tilman's photograph showed less than Mallory's, but he thought the west cwm 'an unpleasant and dangerous place for an advanced base.'

While the Himalayan Committee were not enthusiastic they allowed themselves to be persuaded. Our argument was that since no one had seen the west slope of the south col, and since the icefall, nasty as it looked, bore no mark of impossibility, immediate reconnaissance was needed. Our expedition was organised in less than six weeks. Eric Shipton joined us in July and agreed to lead. The New Zealanders, Hillary and Riddiford, joined later en route. In August we set off, and on 29 September, a week after the close of the monsoon, pitched our base camp at 18,000 ft on the Khumbu glacier between Pumori and Everest.

The reconnaissance that ensued left me with three vivid after-images, each unfaded to this day. The first two came when we climbed on to

An intriguing diversion – 'Abominable Footprints' found by the 1951 party. The right hand picture shows the scale.

Foot of Khumbu icefall from the west.

Pumori and looked back over the Khumbu. Everest startled me not by its height – since the mind failed to grasp the scale – but by the immensity of its mass, for that was enough to astound the eye even without the aid of understanding. The whole north and west faces were open to us: from Pumori, not the 'brutal mass' that Longstaff saw from Tibet, but a sculptured work worthy of the world's highest peak. The ridges of Nuptse jerked up in raw zig-zags to a spiky top, snow-fluted on their flanks and hung with glaciers. A vast cleft split the mountain off from Everest, and through it we could see Lhotse, diamond-shaped but dwarfed. From close under its rock crown, a glacier poured down the west face to the floor of the cwm, and, swollen there from the walls of Everest and Nuptse, burst through the cleft and tumbled to the Khumbu glacier.

The second lasting image was our first sight of the west cwm, for these were most exciting hours as Lhotse and the south col and the west cwm slowly crept into view as we climbed. The history of the mountain (and the destinies of many men) would be affected by what we saw. We could hardly believe our good fortune when all was at last clear. From the top of the icefall the glacier did not run flat as everyone had feared, but rose more than two thousand feet in wide steps leaving less than three thousand feet to the col, whose slopes seen *en face* were not too steep. They were free of stonefall and avalanche menace. They were climbable.

Our immediate concern now was the icefall,

Opposite: The icefall from the north-east spur of Pumori.

In the icefall.

EVEREST *Günter and Norman Dyhrenfurth*

Earth's highest mountain (29,028 ft) has been fought over for nearly half a century. Between 1921 and 1967 twenty-one large expeditions and five small undertakings, a total of twenty-six groups – not counting the numerous aerial crossings – made the 'Third Pole' their goal, at first from the northern or Tibetan side, and after the Second World War mostly from the south, i.e., from the Khumbu glacier in Nepal. Here a British expedition led by Eric E. Shipton in 1951 carried out valuable reconnaissance work, although it failed to gain entrance to the strange sanctuary of the west cwm.

This problem was solved in 1952 by the Swiss who, in the spring and then again in the autumn, fought their way up through the treacherous and wildly broken-up Khumbu icefall to reach the cwm and, beyond it, the south col (26,201 ft) between Everest and Lhotse. The team of Raymond Lambert and Tenzing Norgay pushed on to a height of about 27,900 ft on Everest's south-east ridge, almost as high as Edward Felix Norton's famous lonely attempt on the north face, on 4 June 1924, which ended at 28,120 ft. If it had not been for serious failure of their oxygen apparatus, the men of the Swiss pre-monsoon team might very well have reached the south peak of Everest (28,741 ft). The following November the mountain defended itself with its most irresistible weapon: bone-chilling cold and violent storm.

1953 was the year of decision. There is no need to describe the carefully prepared and perfectly organised large British expedition led by Col.

Opposite: A notable contrast with the ice and snow of Everest – the granite of the Trolltind Wall.

The top of the icefall.

Tenzing and Hillary start from advance base camp for the successful assault.

John Hunt (now Lord Hunt). Its accomplishments are known throughout the world. The first ascent of Mount Everest on 29 May 1953, by Edmund P. Hillary from New Zealand and Sherpa (or rather Bhotia) Sirdar Tenzing Norkey, was a starlit hour of mankind and a classic example of team-work.

The International Himalaya-Expedition 1955, composed of Swiss, Austrians and Americans, reconnoitred the approaches to Lhotse (27,923 ft), Everest's smaller neighbour. Since permission for the undertaking had been granted too late for a pre-monsoon attempt, an unusually long monsoon and premature winter storms prevented the team from reaching the summit. The Austrian Ernst Senn pushed on to a height of about 26,300 ft beneath the entrance to the great couloir, before the onslaught of winter called a halt to all further attempts. Of equal importance to the expedition's progress was extensive work in the fields of cartography, still photography and documentary film production. Norman G. Dyhrenfurth, a member of the Swiss Everest Expedition in the autumn of 1952, was the organiser and leader as well as the film-maker on this undertaking. Erwin Schneider, official cartographer of the Austrian Alpine Club, master of terrestrial photogrammetry, created the outstandingly accurate 1:25,000 scale map of the Everest group, a cornerstone in Himalayan exploration.

1956 was the year of the Swiss. A large expedition – well prepared by the Swiss Foundation for Alpine Research, under the outstanding leadership of Albert Eggler and composed of a team of

Opposite: The formidable final ridge of Everest taken from the South Summit at 9 am on 29 May 1953.

1963 Camp 11 at 21,450 ft – portion of West Ridge visible.

Bernese climbers with exemplary *esprit de corps* – became one of the most successful undertakings in the history of Himalayan mountaineering. The first ascent of Lhotse was made by Ernst Reiss and Fritz Lucheinger on 18 May, using the great couloir of the north-west face as *direttisima*. The second ascent of Everest followed on 23 May, by Jürg Marmet and Ernst Schmied, while Adolf Reist and Hans Rudolf von Gunten made the third ascent on 24 May. They encountered beautiful weather, perfect snow conditions, and found themselves on top physical form. Two windless hours on the summit – an almost incredible stroke of good fortune – resulted in a magnificent photographic record. Although they stopped to collect rock samples, the descent of nearly 3,000 ft to the south col took only two hours!

The First Indian Everest Expedition of 1960 fared far worse. After having established Camp 7, their assault camp, on the south-east ridge in good weather on 24 May at about 27,560 ft, the men were forced to turn back the following morning at a height of 28,300 ft in the face of very strong wind, bitter cold and blinding snow plumes. And yet their competitors, the Chinese Everest Expedition 1960, claimed to have reached the summit of Everest via north col and the north-east ridge during the night of 24 May to the 25. Once there, they hoisted a red flag and placed a bust of Mao Tse-tung on the summit snow, weighted down by rocks picked up during the ascent. In the dark of night they were unable to take pictures, but a photograph taken 'at about 8,700 metres' was published and offered as proof, thus starting a lively and voluminous discussion in various mountaineering journals. Detailed examinations and calculations led to the conclusion that the photograph in question

Opposite: The Lhotse face – South Col and Geneva Spur to left off the picture.
Overleaf: The icefall in '63.

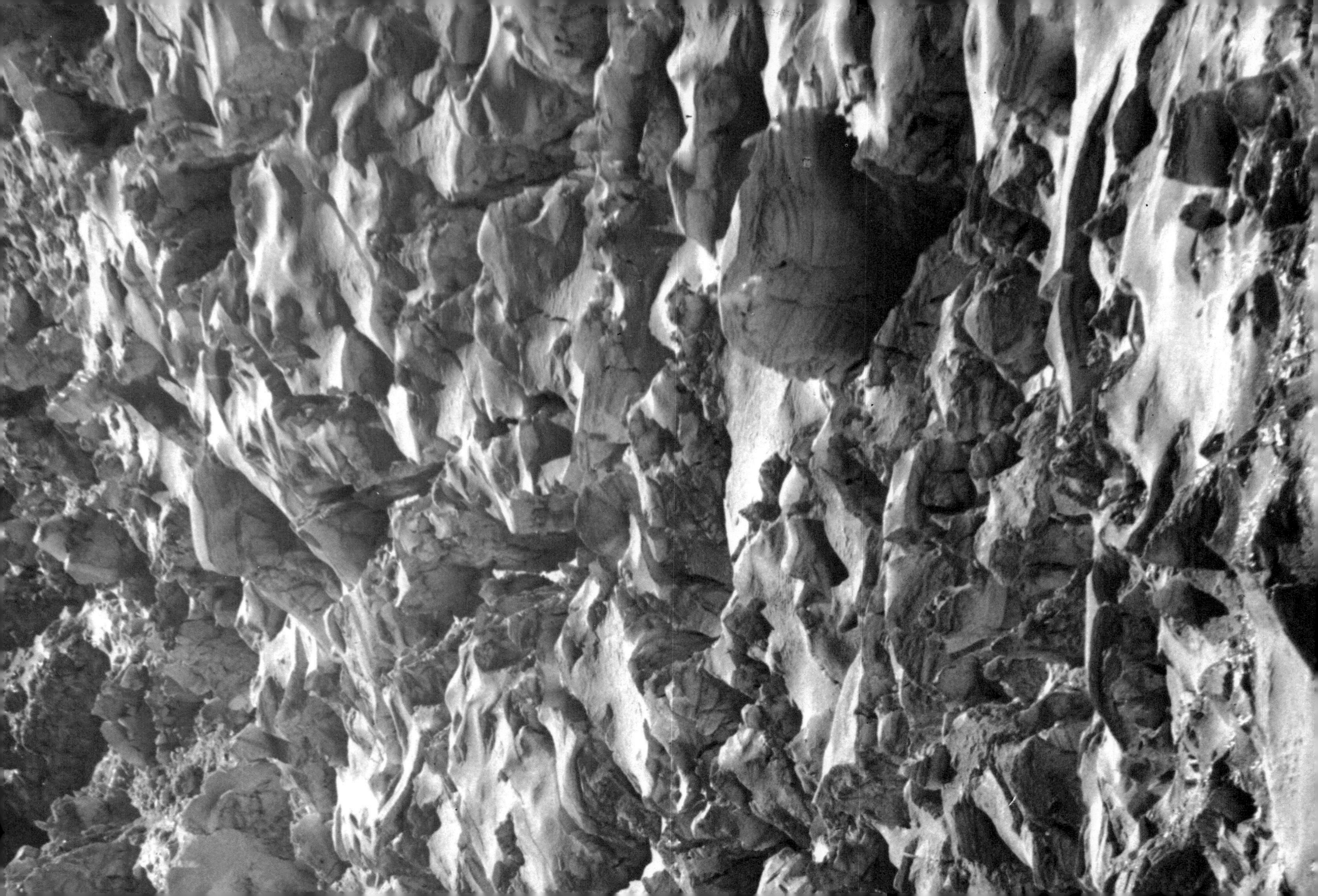

was not taken with a still camera, but rather that it was an enlargement of a single frame from the Chinese documentary film made while establishing camps on the mountain, which was also shown in London in October 1962. The approximate height of the cameraman's position was about 8,500 metres, and not 8,700, as claimed. Then there were other discrepancies: no foreground; an obvious error in the time of day when the picture was taken; contradictions between Indian and Chinese weather reports; an utterly vague route description, etc. It is therefore reasonable to assume that the Chinese mountaineers of the 1960 attempt did reach a point on the north-east ridge somewhere between the 'First' and 'Second Step', but that the summit of Everest was not attained.

The Second Indian Everest Expedition in May of 1962 had no better luck with the weather and was forced to give up before reaching the south peak. Then came 1963, another important Everest year:

The American Mount Everest Expedition 1963 (AMEE), organised and led by Norman G. Dyhrenfurth, reached the summit three times: at 1 pm on 1 May, James Whittaker and Nawang Gombu (Tenzing Norkey's nephew) set foot on earth's highest point, having waged a bitter battle against cold and storm as they fought their way up the south-east ridge. Norman Dyhrenfurth and Ang Dawa IV, his faithful Sherpa friend of four previous expeditions, carried heavy motion picture equipment to a height of about 28,250 ft, just below the final

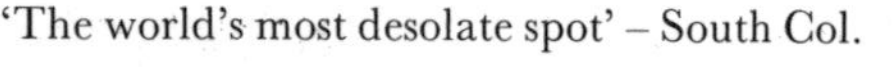

'The world's most desolate spot' – South Col.

steep rise to the south peak. After weeks of storms and subsequent redeployment and renewed build-up of the high camps, Barry Bishop and Luther Jerstad followed the route taken by the first team and reached the top at 3.30 pm on 22 May. Their ascent was part of AMEE's overall strategy of placing men on the summit from near-opposite sides of the mountain. William Unsoeld and Thomas Hornbein – with magnificent backing from a strong support team headed by Barry Corbet – negotiated the difficult and hitherto untried west ridge, and at 6.15 pm on 22 May they, too, stepped up to 'Big Jim' Whittaker's flag-pole. Then they descended the south-east ridge in the other team's footsteps, making the long-cherished dream of traversing one of the great Himalayan peaks come true. In total darkness they joined Bishop and Jerstad who had waited below the south peak, and together the exhausted and oxygen-starved men groped their way down toward Camp 6. Their unavoidable bivouac at a height of 28,000 ft, without tent, sleeping-bags, or oxygen, established an involuntary world record. The temperature hovered at 18 degrees below zero. In the usual Everest weather not one of the four men might have survived this highest bivouac ever spent on a mountain. But Chomolungma, the 'Goddess-Mother,' was kind, and in the early hours of darkness the wind dropped. The following morning Dr David Dingman and Sherpa Girme Dorje came up from Camp 6 with fresh oxygen cylinders and helped the severely frostbitten men down the mountain. For a detailed

Late afternoon at Camp III at 22,900 ft in '63.

The height of achievement

Makalu and Kangchenjunga from the South Summit of Everest.

Everest

The nature of the West Ridge.

South Summit of Everest from West Ridge. Taken on the first traverse of the mountain and the first ascent of the West Ridge by Unsoeld and Hornbein on 22 May 1963 – the climax of a highly successful expedition.

account of AMEE the reader is referred to James Ramsey Ullman's *Americans on Everest* (J. B. Lippincott) and Thomas F. Hornbein's *Everest: The West Ridge* (Sierra Club, San Francisco).

The Third Indian Everest Expedition of 1965, led by M. S. Kohli, was every bit as large and ambitious an undertaking as AMEE: there were nineteen members of the climbing team, ten of whom had been to Everest at least once, if not twice. During the latter part of May an unusual stretch of ideal weather was exploited to the fullest. Nawang Gombu succeeded in making his second ascent of Everest, and between May 20 and 29 a total of nine men in four teams reached the summit by way of the south-east ridge. India has every reason to be proud of this magnificent achievement.

1966 brought Chinese mountaineers back to the mountain, apparently to present to the world – after the rather doubtful results of 1960 – undeniable proof of a spectacular victory. According to scanty reports, however, the men of the Second Chinese Everest Expedition fared far worse than their predecessors. For a long time there was nothing to be learned about their fate. Not until the spring of 1967 did word leak out via Calcutta that the team of twenty-six men had been very scantily equipped, without special clothing and protection against the cold. Two half-frozen men returned to base-camp after only two days. The rest refused to retreat; in Mao's name they continued the assault. Apparently this is what they are still doing. In any case nothing further has been seen or heard of them.

Opposite: The summit of Everest – 6.30 pm 22 May 1963. Note the shadows of Everest, Makalu and Lhotse, then Makalu itself.

Everest from the summit of Nuptse.

AFTER EVEREST *T.S.Blakeney*

Since the first ascent of Everest in 1953 there has been a great upsurge of effort to climb the highest remaining peaks in either the Himalayas or the Karakoram. There is, indeed, too much to record in any detail. To the world at large, Everest was the dominating mountain achievement in 1953, but mountaineers everywhere recognized the outstanding performance of the late Hermann Buhl when, on 3 July, he made, alone, the first ascent of the long-attempted Nanga Parbat (26,660 ft).

1954 saw the downfall of two more of the mystic 8,000 metre peaks, when the Italians climbed K2 (28,250 ft), the second highest peak in the world, and Dr Tichy's party accounted for Cho Oyu (26,750 ft). In the same month (October) as the last-named climb, the French made the first ascents of two 25,000-footers, in Makalu II and Chomo Lonzo, a foretaste of their still greater triumph in 1955 (15 May) when they gained a brilliant success on Makulu itself (27,824 ft), whilst ten days later Kangchenjunga, third highest summit of the world, fell to a British party.

In 1956 the Japanese, most industrious of explorers and climbers in the Himalayas, won to the top of Manaslu, another 8,000 metre peak, and in the Karakoram Gasherbrum II (26,360 ft) was climbed by F. Moravec and party. This same year saw the first ascent of one of the most dramatic-looking peaks in the Karakoram, the Muztagh Tower, (23,860 ft) by a British party, with French rivals close on their heels. Broad Peak (26,400 ft) went to Hermann Buhl,

Southern buttress of Cho Oyu.

Diemberger and others, in 1957; the often-attempted Rakaposhi (25,550 ft) in 1958 fell at last to M. E. B. Banks and Tom Patey, and the same year saw the Americans on top of their first 8,000–er, Gasherbrum I, and Walter Bonatti almost won to the 8,000 metre mark on Gasherbrum IV (26,180 ft) a few weeks later.

1960 was a rich year; Diemberger and others scored the greatest triumph of all, by the first ascent of the redoubtable Dhaulagiri (26,810 ft); Annapurna II (26,041 ft) went to Grant, Bonington and the famous Sherpa, Ang Nyima; and a variety of parties made ascents of Himal Chuli (25,801 ft), Distaghil Sar (25,868 ft), Masherbrum (25,660 ft) and Trivor (25,328 ft). Even more interesting than these higher peaks, however, was the success of the Chinese party led by Pai Chiu-lsiao on the mysterious Amne Machin, once thought to be higher even than Everest, but now written down to 23,491 ft.

1961 saw Everest's great satellite, Nuptse (25,726 ft), climbed by Dennis Davis and others, a mountaineering feat that the climbers, no mean judges, considered really difficult even by the high standards of rock climbing current today. 1962 saw Saltoro Kangri (25,400 ft) as the highest new summit climbed, but undoubtedly the outstanding success of this year was the ascent of Jannu (25,294 ft) by the French.

Finally, and to end the survey, on 2 May 1964, the Chinese climbed the last of the 8,000 metre peaks, Shisha Pangma (Gosainthan): all the 'giants' of the Himalaya-Karakoram had fallen in the short space of fourteen years.

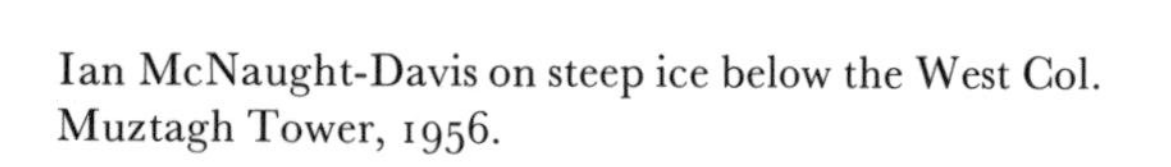

Ian McNaught-Davis on steep ice below the West Col. Muztagh Tower, 1956.

MUZTAGH TOWER *J.M.Hartog*

The Muztagh Tower (23,860 ft) in the Karakoram Himalaya was climbed for the first time in 1956 by a guideless party of four men from Britain. Before then the mountain had acquired a worldwide reputation as impossible, on account of a famous photo taken years before and often reproduced, showing the Tower with two sheer sides and no apparent breaks; this view had even appeared in one semi-authoritative book over the words 'Nature's Last Stronghold'.

Of course people once thought the same about the Matterhorn in Switzerland, whose first ascent last century made such an impression, symbolising a break through the impossible. The leader of the first party to reach the top of the Matterhorn was Edward Whymper, urged on by his passion for the mountain, and by the knowledge that on the other side of the peak there was a rival party (from Italy) also trying their luck. At the summit first, Whymper hurled rocks down the Italian side, and frightened the Italians who returned to their village, before setting out again successfully two days later.

Our team had this all in mind when we were on the Muztagh Tower, for there was a very experienced French party on the other side of the mountain, led by Guido Magnone, an outstanding figure in the contemporary climbing world. We only heard of this by letter after we had started the climb, with information that they had followed us up the Baltoro glacier some days later, and had now gone round to the other side of the mountain – in fact to the way we had intended to try if our first choice turned out to be

Opposite: Leaving the first ice cave; Eiger Direct, Winter 1966.

impracticable. 'Perhaps we can do a Whymper . . .' it was suggested.

It didn't turn out quite that way. Technically our route in the upper section of the mountain above 6,000 metres became quite hard, mostly III with some IV, not allowing for the outrageous exposure with drops of two and four thousand feet on the two sides of our ridge. Since the faces were sheer, the exposure increased in direct proportion to the additional height gained. The French were out of sight, separated from us by a side ridge, and we knew they would have problems too, but had no means of knowing how quickly or easily they would overcome them.

On our side, above an initial 2,000 ft ice slope (III, IV and three pitches of V) to reach the col, the ridge towered up, with one steep 100 ft cliff across it, then another. The first cliff was turned by Joe Brown on the south rock face (IV), the second was turned by Ian McNaught-Davis up a very steep snow couloir (IV–V). The only safe way to ensure one's descent in bad conditions was to equip the route with fixed rope and pitons, and this we had done over all the worst sections lower down, but not above our highest camp. McNaught-Davis and Joe Brown having reached the west summit on 6 July, it was up to Tom Patey and me to reach the true (east) summit the following day. One last rock slab, about 10 ft high, barred the way. Tom led this pitch of V, and pushed me in front to lead the final 150 ft section of snow arête, with still the fantastic exposure, of 6,000 ft on one side and 8,000 ft on the other. This was ridge climbing with a vengeance.

The indifferent weather had discouraged the French, who had considerable trouble in the lower part of their route, and they too had been equipping the worst sections with fixed rope, and

Opposite above: A minor peak above the Baltoro glacier.
Opposite below: Mingbo airstrip (15,500 ft) used during the 1960–1 Scientific Expedition. Taweche in background.

Joe Brown on an exposed traverse out onto the South Face, Muztagh Tower.

South Face and West Ridge of Muztagh Tower. The Hartog route ran from the rock island in the middle of the glacier (Camp II to the right of the rock) thence to Camp III on the level portion of the ridge. The South-East Ridge climbed by the French party is plainly visible on the right, their top camp being on the ice shelf below the East Col.

were ferrying up their stores. One of them emerged from the tent in their upper camp during a break in the weather, and took up his binoculars to scan the culminating summit section, a couple of miles distant. Then two black specks walked into the field of view up that last snow arête. We shouted, but no sound came back. We knew that they had seen us because through our binoculars we could see black specs appear beside the two larger dots that were their tents. For the first time man had been seen on a Himalayan summit. The gigantic scale had always prevented this before.

We came down, abseiling the pitch below the summit, and the 100 ft cliff at 6,300 metres. Below the col there was no time to lose, the mountain was falling down. In the early part of the summer when we had started up, as soon as we had dared after the winter and spring snow had avalanched off, the rocks were plastered together with ice. Now it was thawing and the vertical cliffs facing south were loosing debris of all sizes up to a few tons.

Tom and I were slightly frostbitten, and glad of the fixed ropes. In our higher camps we were both rather ill from drugs we took to alleviate the trouble, and lower down I found myself rather lame. Mac and I came down from the col together and had a right old time dodging those falling rocks. Luckily neither was hit, but Mac lost his iceaxe, and his rucsac was hit while we were on the 2,000 ft ice slope. (Angle measured by instrument was 47° on average!) Prancing round in crampons, we understood what we were

Opposite: East Summit of Muztagh Tower from the (lower) West Summit. K2, eight miles away, rises another 4,000 ft.

Tom Patey nearing the East Summit of the Muztagh Tower.

about, for although amateurs our standards were professional.

When we got down to our base camp I wrote a letter to Magnone and sent it round by porter (3 days' march) with a tin of Scotch shortbread, telling the French of our success, wishing them well, and suggesting they could traverse the mountain as we had left all our fixed ropes in place. They replied inviting us to join them for a celebratory dinner at our base depot.

We had had our measure of climbing now, and were all content with one mountain for that season. Three days later the French arrived and we were delighted to see them. They, too, had all reached the top, a week after us, and found it difficult, too, but apparently it wasn't quite as sensational as our route. Each party knew enough of each other's language for us to chat. They were four climbers, two of whom were guides, and a doctor with a large medical supply kit, but no patients. So Dr Francois Florence took charge of Tom and myself, and started injecting antibiotics into my posterior, thus certainly saving my feet, and most likely my life, from the spreading infection. He decided I should not walk, so I was carried by our porters and the French on an improvised stretcher or on piggyback until we reached a river where we embarked on goatskin rafts for Skardu and its airstrip.

Magnone wrote afterwards that our ascent was the start of alpinism in the Himalayas. Perhaps this is an over-statement. It certainly marked an advance in the type of climb contemplated. Although ours was not the first of the small parties it did at least confirm the pattern when a small private expedition climbed a Himalayan giant which, though not in the top ten for height alone, is still in the top ten for height-plus-difficulty. Everyone got to the top. No lives were lost. No loads or stores were lost. The total cost was just 6% of the successful Italian Expedition the year before to K2.

On the issue of rivalry, we had become friends with the French, because both teams had a great respect for each other, had been through the same hardships, and had had similar fun; we had all emerged without bitterness, but with some understanding of what holds men together. One cannot describe it in words. Although we all see each other from time to time, we do not talk about it. It exists in deeds, in goodwill, and not in writing.

'A Whymper's eye' view down the South-East Ridge from the summit. French Camp IV circled, Younghusband glacier far below.

John Harlin – a portrait by Bonington which captures not only Harlin's undoubted toughness but something also of his aestheticism.

EIGERWAND *Christian Bonington*

The Eigerwand rears like a huge tombstone above the village of Grindelwald on the northernmost edge of the Alps. It certainly ranks as the most notorious mountain face in the world, for no other has excited so much controversy and, at times, downright hysteria, as this six thousand foot wall of stone-wracked ice and rock. As a result it is difficult to get the face into its true perspective, to determine whether it is a magnificent mountain challenge or 'an obsession for the mentally deranged' as Colonel Strutt, editor of the *Alpine Journal*, described it in 1938.

One might question whether it would have achieved such notoriety if it had been tucked away at the end of a glacier in the heart of the mountains, hidden from all but the mountaineer. Instead, it is the perfect stage for melodrama, with a huge, easily accessible auditorium – the stalls in Alpiglen, the circle round Kleine Scheidegg and the royal box for the privileged on the roof of Fritz von Almen's Kleine Scheidegg Hotel, where one can watch the death pangs of the Eiger's victims through the lens of a high-powered telescope. Today, with communication satellites and television, the entire world can watch the play being acted out.

Inevitably this weight of publicity has threatened every climber venturing on to the face with the accusation of being a sensation seeker. In some cases this has perhaps been true, but in the vast majority the climber has attempted the face for its merit as a mountaineering problem. There is no other face in the Alps that combines such size, complexity of route-finding and objective

Opposite: Winter aerial view of the Eigernordwand: 1-First Band; 2-First Icefield; 3-Second Icefield; 4-Flatiron; 5-The Pillar; 6-The Spider.

6
5
4
3
2
1

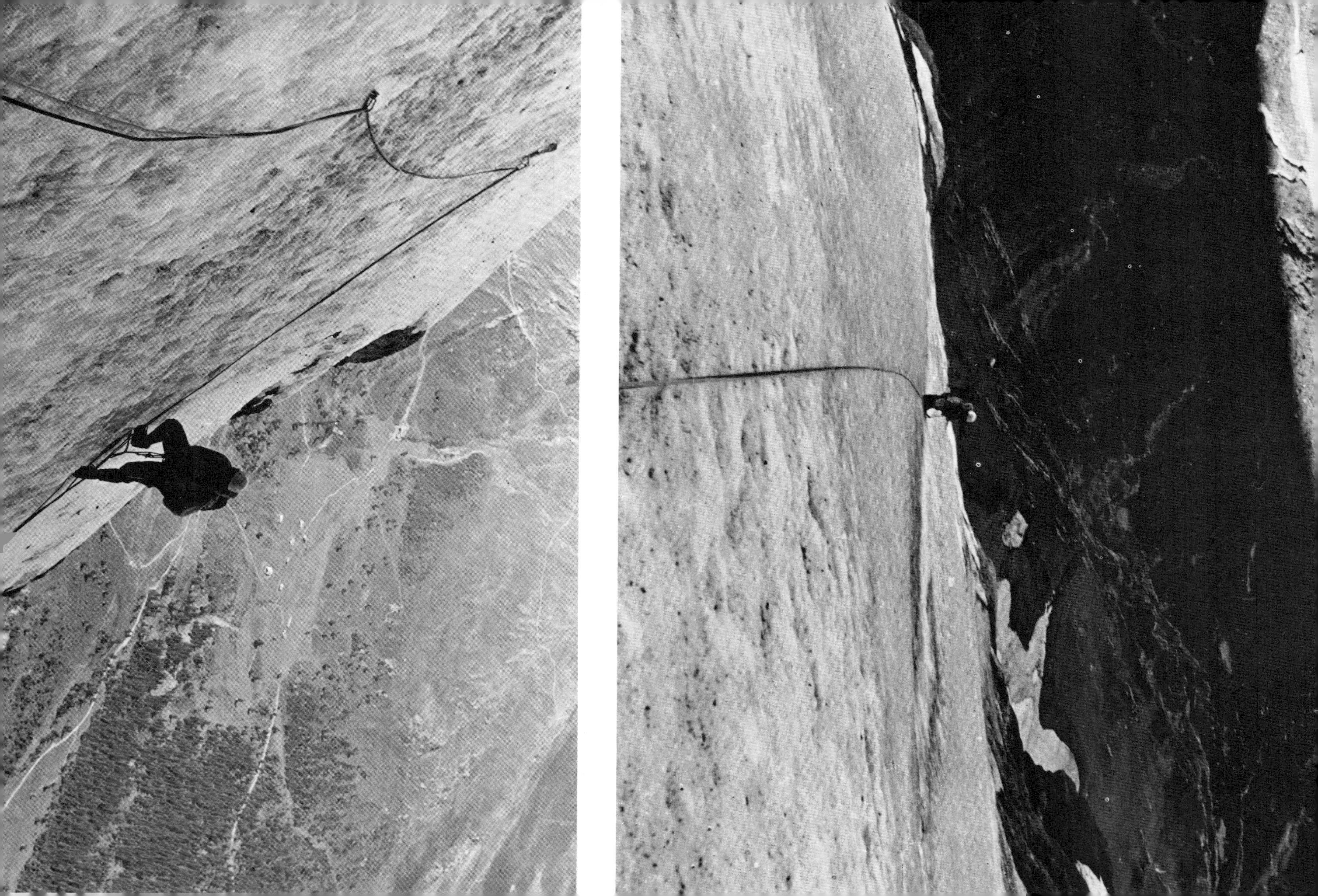

Bonington and Clough's ascent of the Eigerwand in 1963. *Top left:* Bonington on Second Icefield. *Bottom left:* Bonington on Third Icefield. *Left:* Bonington on the White Spider. *Above:* Clough solos up the summit ice. Shortly after the picture was taken the rope was put on again.

Eigerwand, 1962.

Opposite: A 300 ft abseil down the side of the pillar above Death Bivouac, Winter 1966.

Clough at bivouac below difficult crack, 1962.

Brian Nally about to be rescued (by Bonington and Whillans) at the end of the Second Icefield, July 1962. His companion, Barry Brewster, had fallen when climbing the Flatiron the previous day. Secured by Nally all night he was swept to his death shortly before the photograph was taken. This tragedy provided a grim introduction for Bonington to this great face and it says much for his determination that he and Ian Clough a month later became the first British pair to climb it.

Another Eiger tragedy: Tom Carruthers and his Austrian companion Moderegger seen alive for the last time as they tackle the Second Icefield. The short shadows far below emphasise their lateness and suggest that they must have been exposed to stonefall from the White Spider throughout the most dangerous hours of the day.

danger. By modern standards the technical difficulty of the north face route is not great – but it is this very fact that has lured so many climbers to their deaths. Nowhere is the ice steeper than 55° or the rock harder than Grade V (the top grade is VI). A competent climber of average experience should be able to cope with either of these problems, but the Eiger has so many hidden defences. The combination of all these makes it one of the most exacting tests that any mountaineer can face. Brian Nally, after being rescued from the face in 1962, when his companion had been swept to his death, admitted

> It's a pig of a face, but somehow it's the final test of how good you are. . . . now I know that it is better than us.

There are three factors that make the Eigerwand such a challenge. It is on a bigger scale than other Alpine faces. There are no obvious lines of weakness leading to the top, and the route first made by Heckmaier, Vorg, Kaspereck and Harrer in 1938 meanders back and forth for 10,000 ft, seeking the easiest line between the bands of smooth, sheer limestone. It is all too easy

Dougal Haston on fixed rope below the First Band. Winter ascent of the 'direttissimo'.

Layton Korr leads a pitch on the First Band, belayed by Haston – 'direttissimo'.

to make a mistake and waste precious time in getting back on route.

Speed is a vital factor in climbing the Eiger safely, for the weather on the face is particularly unpredictable. It is possible to lie sun-bathing in Grindelwald and watch a puff of cloud form in the amphitheatre of the White Spider, high on the face. From below, it looks innocent, even pretty, but if one was in the Spider at the time, one might be struggling for life itself in the teeth of a violent local storm.

But by far the greatest danger is that of falling stones. Every ledge in the upper part of the face is piled high with scree. If it freezes at night, this is held captive by ice and the face is silent; climbers can venture across its exposed ice fields in safety. But in the early afternoon, the sun strikes the upper part of the wall; the ice melts and the stones start to fall. This is not an indiscriminate bombardment, for the entire upper part of the face forms an amphitheatre round the White Spider, and this acts as a funnel that directs the greater part of the stone fall in an intensive fire down the centre of the wall on to the Flatiron and the end of the Second Ice Field. Any climber crossing this danger zone after midday stands a good chance of being hit.

Eight climbers died before the face was even climbed; many have died since, including six as recently as the summer of '67. Viewed in this light there seems good reason for the violence of the criticism that ascents of the Eiger have always excited. But if one examines each accident individually, all too often one discovers that

certain basic mountaineering rules have been broken, that the climber had been too slow and as a result had crossed the stonefall area at the wrong time of day, that he had gone on to the face in bad conditions, or had been inadequately equipped.

Some weak parties, climbing the face in perfect conditions, have reached the top; others, caught by bad weather, have lost their lives. The Eiger allows very little tolerance for mistakes. It is undoubtedly a potentially dangerous face, but this is part of its fascination, for this very danger can be overcome, even cancelled out, if the climb is tackled in the right way, by a strong party. It is the supreme challenge of mountaineering experience and ability and this is why almost all the outstanding climbers of the post-war generation have measured themselves up to it. The famous French climber, Gaston Rébuffat, fought his way up to the face in a severe storm, and afterwards wrote

> It seems to me that the Eiger, climbed in good weather, would have been a lesser achievement. In this case we had committed no folly, no imprudence. We had made every preparation to succeed and we succeeded. Throughout this ascent, this snow and this storm, we had come to recognize from the bottom of our hearts a great sense of fulfilment . . .

In the same way that the original ascent of the Eigerwand marked a definite stage in Alpine history, so also did the ascent of the Eiger Direct in 1966. The term 'last great problem in the Alps' has become an over-used cliché that has been bandied about for many years, with new problems being discovered and solved annually. But the Eiger Direct really was the last great problem of the Alps, for there is no other face or line that can match up to it in either size, technical difficulty or danger.

John Harlin had planned to use traditional Alpine tactics, but these proved inadequate for a climb of such magnitude. The German party, led by Jorg Lehne, had conceived the idea of treating the climb on a Himalayan scale, using fixed ropes, digging snow holes and ferrying up equipment. Both parties had chosen winter to tackle their climb, to avoid the danger of stone fall, and because, in winter, there tends to be longer spells of settled weather – it is a tribute to the quality of modern clothing and down gear that cold has ceased to be a vital factor in determining the success or failure of a climb.

Inevitably these revolutionary methods caused a great deal of criticism in traditional Alpine circles, but then almost every new development in climbing has had the same effect. It is extremely doubtful if the Eiger Direct could have been climbed by any other method in the winter of 1966. To me the greatest value of the climb was the way two parties of different nationalities started the climb in competition with each other and then in the course of the climb united into a single party eventually to overcome the problem. Its tragedy was the death of John Harlin, so very close to success.

It would be dangerous to say that the story of the Eiger is finished. An Alpine style ascent of the Direct route could still be made; it would probably lie to the right of the existing route, out of the line of the worst stone fall, and would be tackled in the early autumn, when the nights are sufficiently cold to still the bombardment but the days are warm enough to allow swift climbing.

The 'Voie Normale' on the north face of the Eiger will remain one of the most magnificent routes in the Alps – in a way it is the supreme test of mountaineering competence. It will continue to claim the lives of those who are too rash or not ready to take the test.

Opposite: Eiger Direct – an extremely difficult ice pitch led by Bonington.

THE OLD MAN OF HOY

Artificial climbing to a very high standard recorded by a skilled team of climbers and television photographers.

Left: Note precarious pitons tied off with bits of sling.
Opposite: View from South-East.
1 First camera position
2 Haston and Crew's bivvy
3 Brown and Patey's bivvy
4 Last camera position at foot of final crack.
▬▬▬▬▬ original route
o o o o South-East Arête
●●●●● South Face

4
3
2
1

Summit party, left to right: Haston, Patey, McNaught-Davis, Brown and Crew.

Hamish MacInnes using a radio camera from the first camera position.

Opposite: Patey 'jumars' up the rope.

ALPAMAYO

The 1966 British Andean Expedition set out with two objects: to climb the virgin North Ridge of Alpamayo and to make a film of the ascent. They succeeded in both objectives: the climb went well after three weeks hard work and the film won awards at the 1967 Film Festival in Trento.

Opposite: The 'Cat-Walk' section of the icefall – although provided by the party with fixed ropes was always a dangerous spot.

Below: Dennis Gray and Roy Smith approaching the icefall below the North Col.

2,000 ft below the summit on the North Ridge above Camp II. One side of the ridge still in dark shadow.

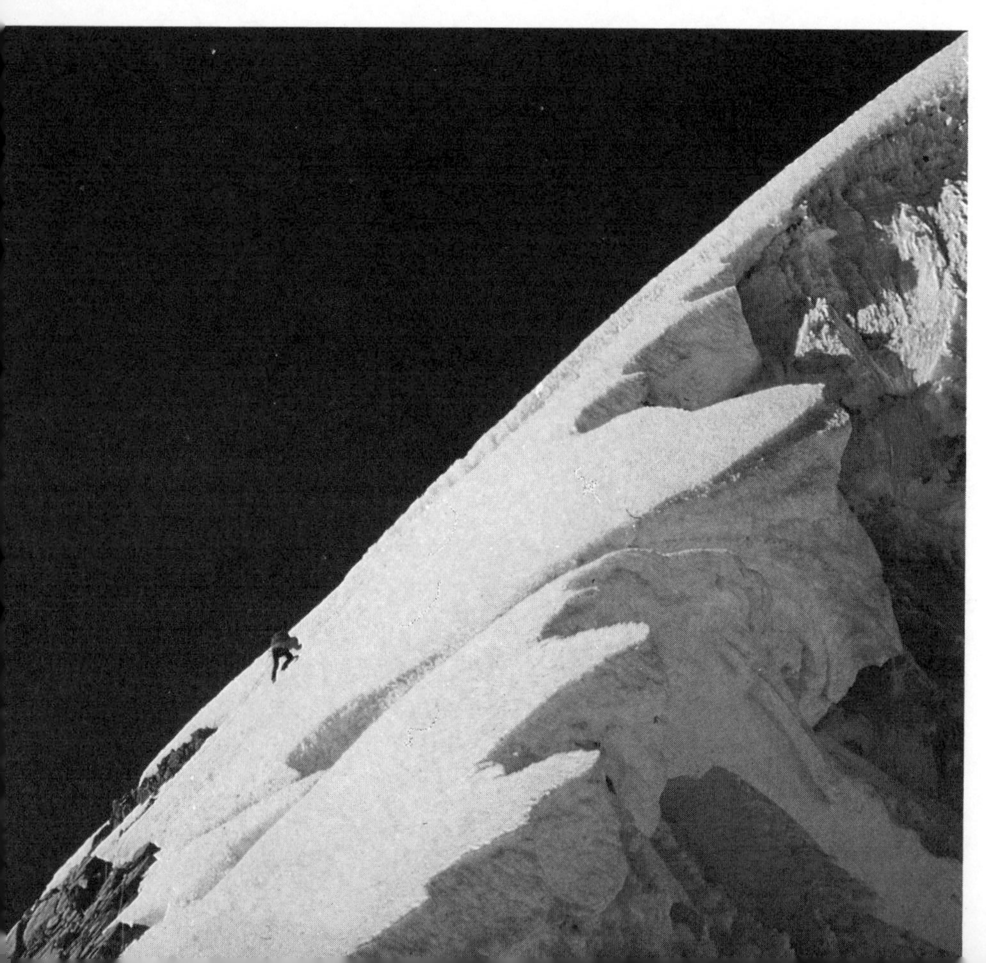

Tele-photo of climbers on the upper snowfields of the North Ridge.

Opposite: Scale – note the size of the figure top left climbing out of the 'Sugar Bowl' section of the icefall.

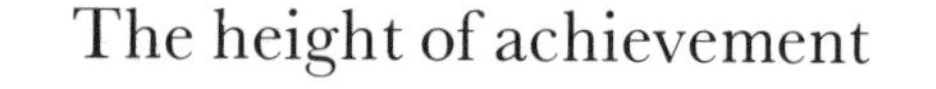

The height of achievement

Opposite: Kelly, the expedition photographer, filming the true summit from the North Summit.
Below: Tele-photo shot from the North Summit. Smith holds the expedition flag aloft on the true summit.

Overleaf, left above: John Amatt near the summit of a subsidiary peak of the Alpamayo ridge during an acclimatisation trip.
Overleaf, left below: Filming the final ascent: Smith (left) and Bathgate.
Overleaf right: Dave Bathgate leaving the site of Camp II on the North Col.

TROLLTIND WALL
ROMSDAL, NORWAY

The Trolltind Wall is an extremely exciting little-known challenge: it constitutes the only vertical mile in Europe and was untouched until Howard, Amatt and Tweedale climbed it in a single push of six days in the summer of 1965. In the summer of 1967 a French party followed a more direct line taking 21 days and making use of some four thousand feet of fixed rope.

Right: For the Trolltind Wall . . . a large ledge. Cracks were very thin and the pitons loose.

Opposite: In the icefall, Alpamayo.

Lower section Trolltind Wall: 3,000 ft overhang above.

Opposite: The greatest vertical wall in Europe – 5,000 ft.
Right: Rusty Baillie 'jumars' up the rope on Sondre Trolltind.

Opposite: A few days before the successful first ascent the same party had spent three days on the face in appalling weather managing to climb only some six hundred feet. After two nights in the same bivouac – the conditions were such as to permit of no movement beyond the confines of the bivouac sack – the effects of exposure forced a final retreat. John Amatt's photograph (and he is to be congratulated upon his hardihood in taking one at all in the circumstances) shows the state of the party as they prepared to move off: wet through, the ropes frozen and covered in grit, exhaustion very near. The descent down rock covered in ice and pouring with water was magnificently led by Tony Nicholls (looking up); the effort took so much out of him that he was unable to accompany the remainder of the party on their sucessful ascent a week later.

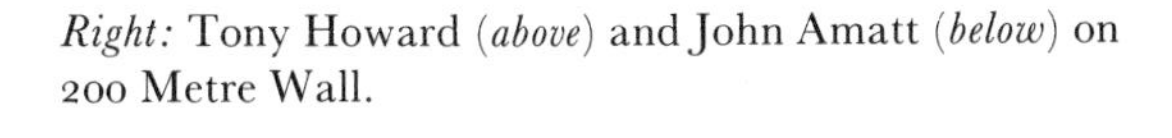

Right: Tony Howard (*above*) and John Amatt (*below*) on 200 Metre Wall.

Chapter 2

The Obverse

Mountain triumphs are won in the face of a host of dangers, both objective and subjective. Here are examples of hazards with which, in addition to the force of gravity, the mountaineer and mountain traveller have to contend

MEDICAL HAZARDS OF THE MOUNTAIN ENVIRONMENT

Michael Ward

Those who wish to succeed must first ask the right preliminary questions Aristotle – *Metaphysics*

Many hazards of the mountain environment are due to the effect of cold, altitude, wind and/or a combination of these factors. An understanding of these hazards has greatly increased the ability of man to live and work safely and satisfactorily under adverse climatic conditions.

At the end of the last century, Tissandier, a Frenchman, and his companions ascended inadvertently without oxygen in a balloon to 28,000 ft. Only Tissandier survived. Yet on Mount Everest ten men on foot have ascended to a similar altitude without harm, being exposed to temperature variations of 100 °F and wind velocities of 100 mph.

The explanation of this seeming paradox and the application of Aristotelian principles forms the basis of success in modern mountaineering at high altitude.

Between 1924, when four men climbed to 28,000 ft without oxygen, and 1952, little progress was made in solving the problem of the last 1,000 ft, although four expeditions went to Mount Everest. This was to a large degree because the true nature of the problem was not fully recognised, so techniques of science, which were opening up new worlds in physics and other fields, were not brought to bear on a comparatively simple problem in applied physiology.

Perhaps the root of the problem lay in the antagonism, more emotional than rational, which every new technique in mountaineering – guide-

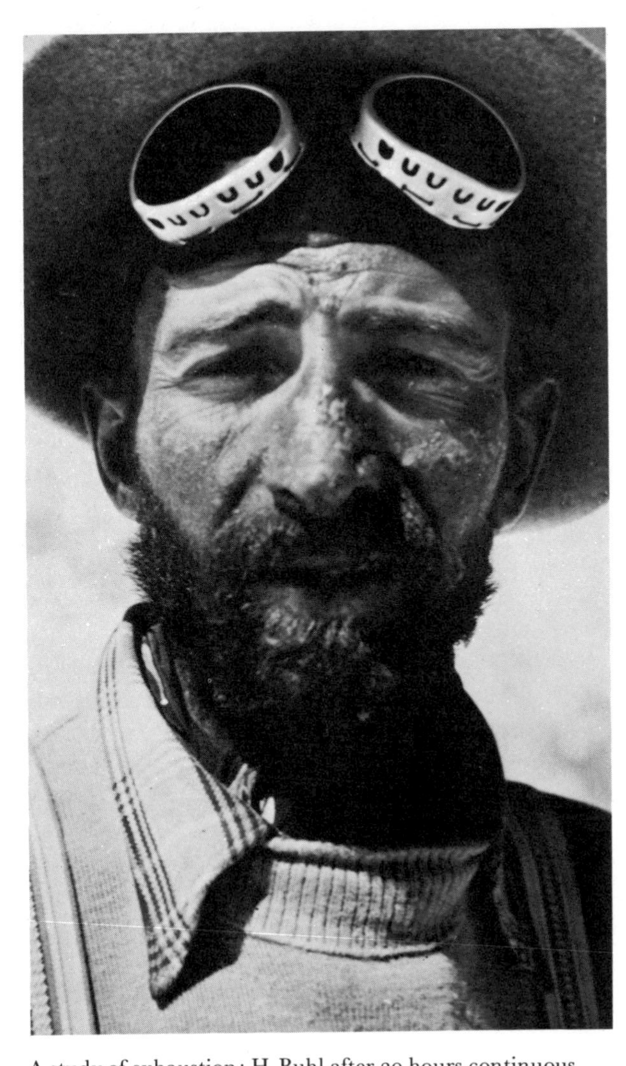

A study of exhaustion: H. Buhl after 30 hours continuous climbing over 22,000 ft on his solo ascent of Nanga Parbat in 1953. He had been forced to bivouac at 26,000 ft.

less climbing, crampons, pitons and oxygen – has aroused. Many climbers passionately believed that in some ways these innovations would diminish their personal stature instead of widening the scope of their craft.

To add to these deeply felt convictions there was the practical consideration that additional oxygen did not seem to provide much added boost at high altitude. There was also some confusion between the findings of experiments in compression chambers, where subjects were exposed to acute oxygen lack, and those of the chronic lack as found while mountaineering at high altitude. It was not until 1952 that it was established that the oxygen flow rate in the past had not been great enough to compensate for the weight of the apparatus. This field research, vital to success on Everest, was carried out by Dr Griffith Pugh.

The solution of this and other problems relating to mundane but fundamental matters of food and fluid intake, boots and clothing, by men trained in the scientific method, has been all-important.

As a result, the range and scope of mountaineering at high altitudes (over 17,500 ft) advanced radically and it is relevant that not only were the world's highest peaks climbed within ten years of the ascent of Annapurna in 1949 by French mountaineers, but also that mountains of technical difficulty similar to those found in the Alps are now being attempted successfully.

The basic feature of all human adaptation is that it is directed towards maintaining the internal environment of the cell. Once the delicate mechanisms which enable the cell to function are disturbed, it dies.

The most important single factor in keeping cells alive is the provision of oxygen. Without oxygen men die in a few minutes and at high altitude oxygen lack is the major hazard.

The basic change is a decrease in the pressure exerted by the air of the atmosphere on the earth's surface, and at whatever height air contains 80% nitrogen and 20% oxygen. At the summit of Everest, the atmospheric pressure, and therefore the pressure exerted by oxygen, is only one third of the sea level value.

It is this pressure that drives oxygen from the air, through the lungs and into the blood, and from the blood to the cells. In the cell oxygen is converted to carbon dioxide and energy is produced for cell function. The carbon dioxide is then transported in the blood to the lungs and exhaled. The body compensates at high altitude by increasing the rate and depth of breathing, by increasing the oxygen-carrying capacity of the blood (oxygen is normally carried in the cells attached to a protein, haemoglobin), by altering the acidity of the blood to enable more oxygen to be carried, and by little understood changes in the cells themselves, whereby various tissue enzyme mechanisms and other factors are brought into play.

It seems likely that the most important mechanism is the last, as individuals with comparable oxygen uptake and haemoglobin concentration do not have the same physical capacity for work at high altitudes.

Another important factor is the maintenance of body temperature. This depends on the correct balance between production of heat by the body, and its loss. Heat is produced by the normal body metabolism which is influenced by the amount of physical effort (itself dependent on the amount of oxygen used). The major heat loss in a cold environment is by convection, or loss by the transfer to air or liquid. Other ways in which heat may be lost are by conduction to the ground or by evaporation due to sweating or through the lungs when panting.

Prevention of loss by convection depends on the insulation provided by air trapped within clothing. If air is stationary insulation is good, but if wind penetrates clothing and disturbs the insulating air there is an increase in heat loss. Good windproof clothing is therefore essential.

In conditions where heat loss is considerable, heat tends to be conserved in the 'inner core' of the body, the brain and trunk, where the vital organs are situated, at the expense of the 'outer shell' – the limbs, skin, fat and muscle. Under normal conditions the temperature of the 'inner core' is 37 °C (98·4 °F), but the temperature of the 'outer shell' may often be below this.

The acclimatisation of man to high altitude is a remarkably effective process, but a long period is necessary for maximum efficiency; say several months at or around 15,000 ft. Above 17,500 ft, however, acclimatisation breaks down and a condition termed high altitude deterioration occurs. Initially this is gradual but it becomes more rapid at greater altitude; thus men have lived for three months at 19,000 ft, whilst two days is the maximum at 28,000 ft without oxygen. Deterioration may be extremely severe, the mountaineer becoming gravely ill.

A number of factors – inadequate food, poor living conditions, cold and wind – increase the rate of deterioration. In the winter of 1960–1 a study of the long-term effects of high altitude were made by a group of scientists and mountaineers from America, Britain, India, Australia and New Zealand working in a hut placed at 19,000 ft in the Everest region. Much of our knowledge of the effects of high altitude dates from this period.

Amongst mountaineers a number of illnesses occur whose sole cause is the environmental factor of cold or high altitude either singly or in combination.

For many years it has been known that when ascending to 8,000 ft and above individuals suffer from nausea, vomiting, headache and other symptoms. Formerly these illnesses were grouped under one general heading of 'mountain sickness'. Several distinct clinical conditions have now been distinguished.

The commonest and best known is acute mountain sickness, known in South America as 'Seroche'. One of the earliest descriptions was given by Father Joseph de Acosta, a Jesuit priest, in 1570, when crossing a pass in the Andes:

I was surprised with such pangs of straining and casting as I thought to cast up my soul too; for having cast up meate, flemgue, and choller, both yellow and greane, in the end I cast up blood with the straining of my stomach.

The onset of symptoms is often delayed by several hours and occurs usually on rapid changes of altitude. Though relatively common, therefore, when ascending by car, train or air, it is less often noted at extreme altitude when ascents are made on foot and there is a less abrupt fall in oxygen tension.

In some individuals the clinical features may be extremely severe and prostrating: others never appear to suffer from acute mountain sickness. Usually the patient recovers within a day or two.

'Chronic mountain sickness', or Monge's disease, occurs rarely in certain dwellers on the South American altiplano at 12,000 ft, who become intolerant to altitude and have to descend.

A particular condition with oedema (or fluid) in the lungs has been described with increasing frequency. Onset may be rapid, the patient becoming gravely ill, and a curious feature of this condition is that it tends to recur when a particular individual returns to altitude. The first recorded case occurred on Mont Blanc (15,800 ft) and was described by Angelo Mosso in 1898. South American physicians, especially Alberto Hurtado, have noted cases in high altitude dwellers; whilst to Charles Houston, the distinguished American mountaineer and physician, must go the credit for bringing this condition to the notice of mountaineers. Cases have been recorded increasingly in the last few years and may be difficult to distinguish from pneumonia. Less serious attacks may be commoner than is generally realised.

The onset of pneumonia may be equally rapid. However, treatment of each condition is similar.

As already indicated, an important adaptive mechanism is the increase in red blood cells. At sea level about 40% of the blood comprises cells, the rest being fluid; however at altitude 65% may be cells, and if further dehydration occurs this figure may for short periods be higher and thus the tendency to thrombosis is increased. Two deaths are known to have occurred on expeditions due to this cause.

Cold injury may be of a general nature, as in exposure, or more localised as occurs in frostbite.

Exposure is not a strict medical term but it is usually used to denote the serious effects of exposure to a cold environment at any altitude. The essential feature of this condition seems to be a reduction in the heat content of the body, and the effects become serious when the 'inner core' body temperature falls. Even at low altitude the combination of fatigue, cold and anxiety or any mental stress is particularly dangerous and, especially in untrained people, may lead rapidly to hypothermia (cooling of the 'inner core'); the greater the altitude the more lethal this combination may become.

Whilst there is some evidence that fatigue may be due to cooling of local muscle groups, there is no evidence that exhaustion is due to a fall in 'inner core' temperature.

It is unusual for experienced mountaineers to suffer from exposure, unless as a result of accident, as they are able to foresee the hazards inherent in the mountain environment and are mentally equipped to deal with a survival situation.

A number of deaths due to exposure occur in Great Britain each year, and the prevalent wet-cold climate is an important factor. Because water is a good conductor of heat, individuals

Silver Hut, 19,000 ft with Rakpa Peak behind. A party of scientists spent from November 1960 to March 1961 working in this hut, carrying out experiments on effects of high altitude on man.

Opposite: Frostbite.
Far right: The same toes nineteen days later after treatment with hyperbaric oxygen.

lose heat in wet clothes. To maintain body heat, therefore, a higher output of energy is essential (i.e. to walk faster), and if for any reason this proves impossible progressive cooling occurs. Changing to dry clothes will maintain heat but this may not be possible.

There is some evidence that women, due to a thicker layer of subcutaneous fat, are better insulated against heat loss and are able to survive exposure better than men. A number of cases have been recorded in which, under similar climatic conditions, women have remained unfrostbitten whilst men have lost fingers and toes from this cause; also women have remained alive in these situations when men have died.

In December 1951, a fit party of four men and one woman set out at night in a snow-shower from a lodge at 1,200 ft in Scotland. They were inadequately clothed and they camped later in the evening. Next morning a gale was blowing and in trying to return to the lodge the four men collapsed consecutively and died within a period of hours. The woman survived.

The mental attitude too of the female is more directed towards survival than that of the male, though paradoxically it is the male who is more likely to get into a 'survival situation'.

In the dry-cold environment of the Polar regions or high mountains, conditions are different and the prevention of sweating and subsequent loss of body heat is important. However, at high altitude excessive physical exertion may be impossible because of oxygen lack and even the maintenance of body heat can be extremely

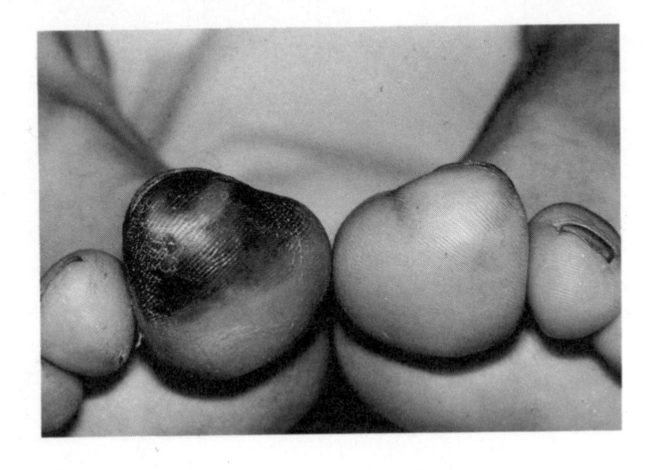

difficult. It is noteworthy that the use of oxygen in these conditions does restore heat to cold extremities.

A number of mountaineers have become frostbitten on Everest despite being both fully clothed and fit. If illness is added to altitude frostbite becomes a near certainty.

Cold air in itself is not so dangerous a freezing factor as cold *and* wind. The chilling effect of a temperature of +20 °F and a 45 mph wind is equal to that of a temperature of −40 °F and a 2 mph breeze.

Frostbite is a condition in which ice-crystals form in the tissues (about 70% of the body-weight consists of water), usually in between the cells. As a result water is sucked from within the cells and the crystals enlarge. The various enzyme and other mechanisms within the dehydrated cells are interfered with, and if they remain in this condition for a period, varying with the type of cell, they die. The blood supply to the affected part also is diminished or abolished. This is part of the body's defence mechanism, as if the blood cooled by the frostbitten tissue is allowed to circulate to the temperature-regulating centre in the brain the 'inner core' temperature would fall and the individual would become gravely ill. Thus the 'part' of the 'outer shell' is sacrificed for the good of the vital organs in the 'inner core'.

The treatment of frostbite may be difficult, as the conditions under which it occurs are climatically severe and access to adequate facilities impossible for a long period. In general, carrying patients with frostbitten lower limbs in the mountains is too time-consuming, so if the climber can walk, even on frostbitten feet, it is better for him to do so. In a number of cases this does not appear to have aggravated the condition.

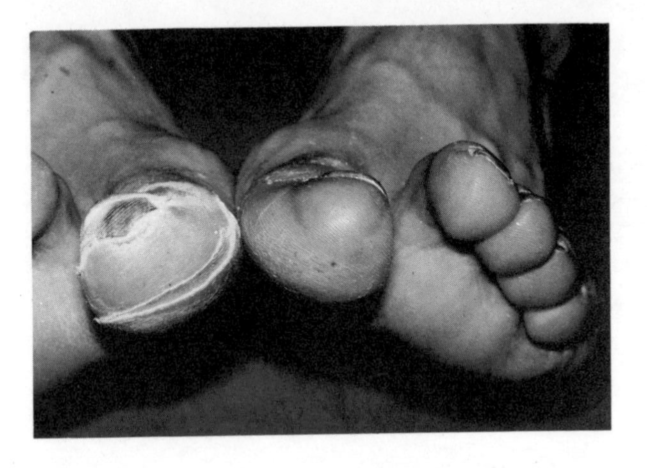

At high altitude, oxygen should be given to increase the oxygen content of the blood that reaches the affected area. In hospital a variety of treatments have been used, and of these rapid rewarming seems most effective. Oxygen at two atmospheres pressure (hyperbaric oxygen) has been also used in four cases with good results. When oxygen is used at increased pressure it dissolves in the fluid part of the blood. This enables more oxygen to get to the damaged cells than would otherwise be possible under sea level conditions.

At high altitude illness or injury and the subsequent rescue may extend the party to its limits. The following was such a case:

Whilst climbing at 26,700 ft on Makalu in 1961 Mulgrew, a fit young mountaineer, suddenly developed an agonising pain in his chest due to thrombosis in the lung and later he began to cough up blood. Descent was slow due to exhaustion and he developed severe frostbite of the legs and hands. A further two nights were spent at 25,000 ft and finally he became unconscious and had to be carried down the mountain on a makeshift sledge of rucksack frames. On several occasions he was thought to have died. He survived but later developed an abcess of the lung and had some fingers and both legs amputated. Today he leads an active normal life, walking extremely well on artificial limbs.

Incidents such as this are very rare, yet that such penalties may be exacted at all is horrifying. The reason why experienced mountaineers are unlikely to be broken or made bitter lies in their commitment, their understanding and acceptance of the risks. However, mountaineering is a sport in which some risk is always present and it is salutary to consider that the mortality rate to climbers (excluding porters),

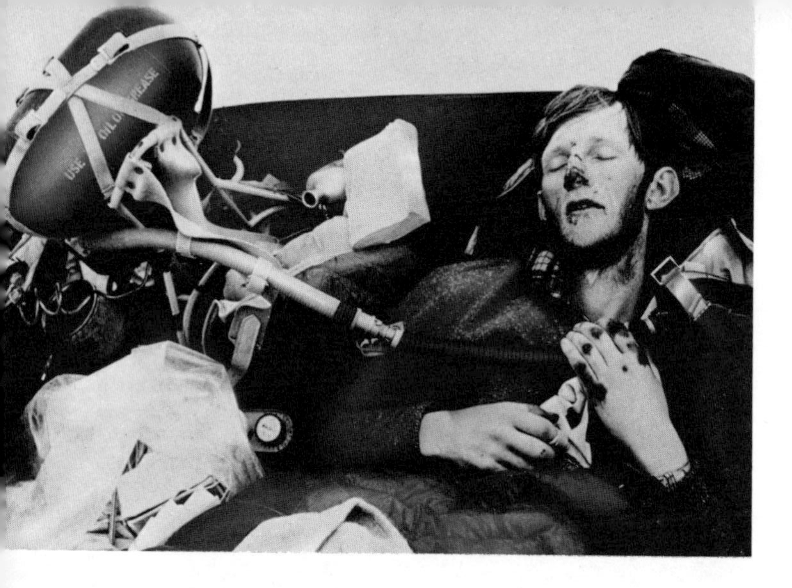

whilst attempting the world's ten highest peaks, is of the order of 7%.

An important factor which has never been given sufficient prominence in mountaineering is the close association between mental and physical symptoms produced by environmental disease.

All the diseases which result directly from extremes of environment can be associated with changes in mental attitude and certain physical and mental characteristics associated with adolescence are likely to increase the hazards. For example a tall thin boy may be more susceptible to hypothermia. Hypothermia in young people may present mental symptoms such as insubordination and lack of communication. Unsteadiness and collapse then follow, and in some cases unconsciousness and death occur within two hours. Even experienced mountaineers suffering from exposure may do alarming things, although the onset is less rapid and unconsciousness and death less likely.

The onset and severity of symptoms may be influenced by the age and experience of the individual in other ways. An inability to regulate energy and strength and to have little in reserve mentally or physically, may lead to dangerous situations. In field sports these tendencies present no problem. In one recent survey in the medical press it was reported that in twenty-three mountain exposure incidents in various parts of the British Isles there were twenty-five deaths out of a hundred persons at risk.

Severe exhaustion may give rise to paranoid symptoms; whilst at high altitude, due to the sensitivity of the brain cells to oxygen lack, an individual may act in a peculiar manner and even become unconscious. Thus in 1953 on Everest, Hunt, after two days at 26,000 ft, had to be escorted from the south col, but was unaware of the severity of his condition at the time. After ascending to a similar height on Makalu the author became unconscious for twenty-four hours on descent to 24,500 ft. An infective illness, such as pneumonia, which interferes with oxygen diffusion through the lungs, may present mental symptoms at high altitude. Such a case occurred in 1961 when a young and extremely fit New Zealand climber suddenly became irrational during the march-in at 15,000 ft. Subsequently he developed the classical features of pneumonia.

It is well known that will-power may mask symptoms and increase performance. However, it must be recognised that lack of resolve, poor memory and poor morale may be distinct clinical features of environmental illness. Misplaced efforts of will, based on insufficient knowledge, may well aggravate a situation. Thus exposure cases suffering from mental symptoms may be made worse by 'pressing on', and collapse accelerated.

The greatest caution should always be exercised in assessing such conditions, especially as in recent years mountaineering has been utilised increasingly by adults who claim that the characters of young people benefit from mountain experience. Many of those involved are unlikely to have a natural affinity or talent for this medium and it is perhaps not surprising that accidents and deaths occur due to acute medical conditions. This is a most disturbing development in modern mountaineering.

The majority of training parties are well conducted and properly constituted, undertaking routes well within their capabilities under good conditions. Nevertheless in the UK 35% of accidents occur in 'guided' parties.

Any organised use of the mountain environment for the 'character training' of minors may

Opposite far left: Makalu 1961. Mulgrew receiving oxygen therapy for frostbite of fingers and pulmonary thrombosis. *Opposite left:* Bicycle ergometer on Makalu Col (24,500 ft). Ward and West are assembling the apparatus which was used for physiological experiments. Everest in the background.

be a dubious expedient beset with moral problems and medical objections. In fact the mountain environment is surely the test of a mountaineer. The specific virtues that may be developed and maintained in this esoteric medium call for a serious individual commitment and a long apprenticeship. The mountains could never be a valid or desirable testing ground for the untried and undedicated.

The qualities of skill, courage and self-reliance specific to mountaineering and displayed by highly qualified climbers are forged in the fires of adversity provided by extreme climatic conditions and on routes of great difficulty.

It follows that the mental and physical attributes necessary to leading mountaineers cannot be developed under the conditions of safety and supervision that should prevail among organised groups of young people. It may be argued, therefore, that it would be in the interests of all concerned if unrealistic claims for 'character building' were dropped in relation to this sport. This should help to eliminate the lunatic fringe who have been known to take children out in weather conditions avoided by experienced climbers.

For the majority, mountaineering provides the benefits derived from physical fitness in country which attracts and inspires them. But mountaineering is not war; it is best done for pleasure, and the decision to climb should be an individual one and never the result of moral pressure or artificial inducement. A mature understanding of all the risks involved enhances the safety of the climber and all who climb with him.

It should be stressed that a proper apprenticeship aims to equip the climber to succeed and to survive. His attitude to life, far from being negative, is an expression of virility and confidence in a natural environment.

Ward and Gill can just be seen on the sunlit and very steep slope just below the summit of the Rakpa Peak. Blood samples were taken before and after the climb to assess fatigue.

Swiss chalets built with lean-to roofs to permit snow slides to pass over them.

THE MENACE OF FALLING MASSES *Colin Fraser*

Rockfalls, and avalanches of snow or ice, are the main natural hazards of the mountains; they are to the alpinist what storms and water-spouts are to the sailor, but they are even more lethal. The effect of these hazards, and their gravity, depend to a large extent upon mountaineering practices and tendencies. For example, in the eighteenth century, when mountaineering was in its infancy, it was usual to climb on snow rather than rock. For this reason, there were many accidents caused by snow avalanches, and some famous climbers died in them.

During the period when the classic rock-ridge routes were being opened, avalanches became less important, but this state of affairs was not to last for long. In the search for new routes, and new conquests, climbers began to probe the defences of the faces. They made, and are still making, first ascents on mountains notorious for their loose rock, ascents which in the past had been considered not only too difficult but also too dangerous because of the frequent volleys of stonefall shots fired by the mountain.

By reason of their geographic formation and weathering, some mountains or faces are more prone to stonefalls than others. During the day, melt water may percolate into fissures and crannies and, since water expands on freezing, the cold of night may disaggregate the rock and loosen stones. The next day's sun will thaw the ice that was binding the masses, and stonefalls will result – hence the increased frequency of stonefalls as the sun's rays warm a face. But apart from these generalities, stonefalls are basically an

Opposite: Cornices on Rottal Sattel.

Line of cleavage, slab avalanche.

entirely unpredictable hazard, and areas where observation shows that they take place regularly have an inherent danger factor that is beyond the climber's control.

Ice avalanches are basically similar in their unpredictability, and in some cases in their origin (i.e. expansion, on freezing, of infiltrated melt water). To climb or cross beneath seracs, therefore, has its built-in element of danger. Although climbers were not involved, the Mattmark disaster of 1965 showed the general wisdom of not loitering or crossing unnecessarily below a glacier. In that case, it was probably the exceptionally heavy summer rainfall that, by gathering in the crevasses and lubricating the underlying rock, caused more than a million cubic metres of ice to break away and kill eighty-eight workmen involved in the construction of a dam. Work had been in progress for five years, and a further two months would have seen it complete.

Ice avalanches, which may also be provoked by glacier movement or by sunshine softening the ice, are particularly frequent and vicious in the Himalayas where many climbers have been surprised by them.

Snow avalanches are fundamentally different from ice avalanches or rock falls in that there is a far smaller element of pure chance in their occurrence. And in most cases when mountaineers are caught by them, it is they themselves who have started them. Generally speaking, skiers are more endangered by snow avalanches than are climbers: boots are less avalanche-provoking than skis, and avalanches in summer are less

Chaukhamba Garhwal: two men lost their lives.

common than in winter. However, if winter climbing expands in the quest of new 'winter firsts', the menace to climbers will also grow, perhaps not on the sheer faces which at present are the main objectives in winter (for they usually are too steep to hold much snow), but at least during the approach or retreat from such faces.

The causes of snow avalanches are now well understood, and even if they remain too complex to allow precise forecasting for a given slope, it is possible to state with some accuracy when there is a general danger, and on what slopes and at what altitude such danger is the greatest. Warning services exist in many alpine countries and bulletins are given out over radio and television and in the press.

The climber is able to protect himself to a great extent by learning about the causes of snow avalanches, by developing his powers of observation, and by learning the important art of selecting the safest possible route once he has decided that danger exists.

Space does not permit a complete explanation here, but, in general terms, an avalanche is brought about by a fracture in the snow cover – a fracture which usually occurs as a result of some structural weakness in the snow cover.

Of particular danger to climbers are slab avalanches, those which break away over a wide area of slope all at once. They occur when a relatively cohesive snow layer, or ensemble of snow layers, is lying on a base to which it is not firmly anchored. This base may, for example, be a layer of loose and fragile crystals lower in the

Powder snow avalanche.

snow cover, or wet grass or rocks. To know that such a weakness exists will help a climber to protect himself. The guide, Maurice Crettex, used to plunge his ice axe into the snow, place his ear to it and say he was listening for avalanche danger. Far more likely was that pushing his ice axe into the snow enabled him to feel for loose layers below the harder ones on top. If he found such a situation, he would be able to take the necessary precautions such as avoiding steep slopes and sheltered areas in which wind-packed snow had accumulated, spacing out his party, moving near the fall-line when possible, etc.

If a mountaineer also knows the various factors that will aggravate the danger, and keeps them in mind throughout the climb and descent, he will be in much greater safety. He should know, for example, that the weight of an additional snowfall increases the stresses in the snow cover and is therefore avalanche-provoking; or that a rise in temperature will weaken the snow and that any subsequent increases in stress, such as that brought about by a climber's weight on a slope, may release an avalanche. And rain, too, heightens the danger, for its weight increases the stresses; it warms the snow, and it lubricates the crystals in the same way as does melt water.

Even the best mountaineers may miscalculate the risk and end up in an avalanche – a life or death predicament. But if they have used their knowledge and powers of observation properly, they will not have been taken entirely by surprise. This will give them a far greater chance of surviving, for, being prepared, they will take the correct action. And if the accident was not totally unexpected, those of the party not carried away are far more likely to remain calm and carry out that vital first search for the victims in the approved way. Since alpinists seldom live for more than two hours in a snow avalanche, time is the all-important factor. Therefore an immediate and systematic rescue action by other climbers present, while just one or two go to the valley for help, is most likely to lead to the *live* rescue of the victim(s). Never should everyone go for help, and even if there is a single survivor only, he should carry out a rudimentary search before going to find reinforcements.

The advent of the supersonic airliner, if it is allowed to fly at supersonic speed over mountain areas, will certainly increase the phenomenon of falling masses. Although it is very doubtful whether normal sounds actually release avalanches, there can be no doubt that the shock wave of a sonic boom will cause teetering masses of rock snow or ice to be dislodged.

Opposite: Ice avalanche: Trugberg, Jungfraujoch.

The emblem of the Mountain Rescue Association of North America and its affiliated teams.

MOUNTAIN RESCUE *George R. Sainsbury*

The Cascade and Olympic mountains of Washington State rise from a few hundred feet above sea-level to an elevation of 8,000 to 9,000 ft. This impressive barrier catches the moisture-laden westerly winds from the Pacific, creating jungle-like rain forests at moderate elevations and heavy glaciation not far above the timber-line. Jutting above the general level of the Cascade range are several volcanoes, the highest of which, Mount Rainier, reaches an elevation of 14,410 ft. With well over 1,000 recognised climbing routes on the several hundred most important peaks in the ranges, it is not surprising that this state was the birthplace of organised mountain rescue in North America.

Occasional rescue efforts occurred during the early days of climbing in the State, but by the 1930's accidents were so frequent that more organisation was called for. Lists of climbers were compiled, screened for competence and availability, and telephone committees formed to call them in case of emergency. Near the close of the Second World War the Mountain Rescue Council was organised, modelled to some extent on European rescue teams, by climbers who had become convinced of the need for a permanent group that could provide training, specialised equipment, and safety education. In Colorado, 1,500 miles to the south-east, the Rocky Mountain Rescue Group was being formed at the same time to meet similar needs on the 14,000 ft peaks of that range.

As the sport expanded, more rescue groups came into being throughout the mountainous regions of Canada and the United States. The Mountain Rescue Association was formed in 1959 to establish standards and disseminate information to rescue units in North America. More than thirty rescue groups now qualify for membership, ranging from Alaska south through western Canada and the western United States to the Mexican border.

Rescue has been revolutionised in North America in the last decade by the development of lightweight transistorised radio equipment and the jet helicopter. During the well-known Mount McKinley rescue in Alaska in 1960 radio communication broke down completely, partially because of the variety of frequencies in use. Following this experience, the Mountain Rescue Association successfully applied for its own emergency frequency, and most contiguous rescue units now enjoy inter-communication on rescues without interference.

While almost any helicopter is likely to be pressed into service for rescue if available, much of the recent work has been carried out by military jet helicopters which are little affected by high altitude. Some of these versatile machines can lift 1,000 pounds at 14,500 ft in almost any atmospheric condition, in contrast to the 4,000 to 6,000 ft ceiling of the non-jet helicopter eliminates the ground effort. The leader of a rescue operation must always assume that weather may prevent a helicopter lift-out, and even in ideal weather it is frequently necessary for skilled climbers to transport the victim to a location where the lift-out can be effected. The dedicated climbing-rescuer will always be the backbone of mountain rescue efforts.

Opposite: The accident took place in 1966 on the North Ridge of Mt Stuart which bisects the picture. Rescue teams were from Seattle and Yakima-Ellensburg. The victim recovered and is climbing again.

The victim being lowered to the pre-selected helicopter lift-off point.

Still being lowered.

Another view from helicopter which has turned through 90 degrees.

Lift-off – cable just visible.

Team member signals helicopter with smoke flare while victim is got ready for lift-off.

Helicopter approaches.

Nearly alongside.

Victim has been winched in next to the door. The helicopter can now land on the first available spot and load him through the back doors for evacuation to hospital.

A MOUNTAIN EPISODE *Charles Houston*

Charlie Houston's story is primarily one of defeat – the summit was not reached and a member of the party lost his life – but it was a noble defeat that bore many of the elements of victory.

That the party were able to extricate themselves from a situation of such appalling danger, and to survive such a fall, was a singular achievement for the corporate spirit of man. It would not have been possible had not each individual member exerted, in the interests of the group as a whole, every last ounce of strength, determination and courage that he possessed.

One can readily understand why Charlie Houston, feeling it would be wrong for an 'I' to intrude into such a narrative, writes in the third person.

The eight men huddled in the storm-torn tents faced a grim prospect. One day earlier their carefully laid plans had seemed almost sure of success. Now, in a short space of hours, they were no longer looking to the final steps to victory but instead were desperately discussing how to save their lives. For six days they had been storm-bound in their highest camp, waiting for a chance to try the summit; now on 7 August one man was mortally ill: with worsening storm they would be lucky to get down alive. All their long efforts had brought them to this high failure and perhaps death.

The eight were members of the third American attempt to climb K2, 28,250 ft high, and 1,000 miles north and west of Everest. Ever since their first party had reached 26,000 ft in 1938, the leaders had dreamed of another try. Dr Charles S. Houston, family physician, and Robert H. Bates, teacher of English, had carried most of the organisational load, but all the others – Robert W. Craig, philosopher; George Bell, physicist; Dee Molenaar, geologist; Pete Schoening, chemist; and Arthur Gilkey, geologist – had helped. Captain Tony Streather of the British army was transport officer, and Colonel M. Ata-Ullah liaison officer with the Pakistan army.

The months of preparation, the flight half way around the world, the march of 175 miles to base camp had all gone smoothly. Two hundred local porters had been enlisted to carry supplies for three months through the country which Kipling called 'beyond the passes', but once at base camp the party relied only on themselves, though they had eight men from Hunza to help stock the lower camps. For five weeks they relayed loads up the route pioneered in 1938. Each lower camp took six or eight days to stock, the higher ones took three or four. In this slow fashion a pyramid of supplies was built so that each camp was left with precious food and fuel for the descent. A thousand feet below the top a camp for two men would be established with supplies for several days to see them to the summit and back, with a reserve in case of storm. . . . These were the plans, this had been the work. On 1 August 1953, they seemed within reach of their goal: six men with twelve days' food and fuel were settled at camp eight at nearly 25,000 ft, with 3,000 ft to climb; two others would join them next day. But trouble began that first night – high clouds, rising wind, and an ominous grey overcast.

At dawn on 2 August clouds enveloped them completely. Visibility was limited and winds beat at them; the temperature was around zero. Through the storm the last two men groped their way up that evening. Now all were together, fit and strong and well supplied. The wind rose during the night. Runs appeared in the fabric of one tent. By a blessing it lasted until daybreak before ripping to ribbons. Houston and Bell dragged their belongings to other tents and crept in. Two men with sleeping bags, air mattresses, stoves, pots, food, clothing are cramped in a small mountain tent, three are very definitely a crowd; but they managed – they had no choice. Unbelievably the wind increased all day. Gusts shook the tents with a sound like thunder – then a lull, then a shattering blast from another direction. They could not talk during the blasts, fine powdery snow sifted over everything, and it was so cold that they wore all their clothing in their special down sleeping bags. Leaving the tent was possible only in brief and unpredictable lulls. They could not keep the stoves lighted, for no matter how they shielded them gusts blew out the flame, already precarious enough at this altitude. So there was no way of getting water, no way to make hot meals. In this frozen desert, surrounded by ice and snow, they might even die of thirst! Eating snow was little help.

Morale was high, and they talked constantly of the summit. No man was dictator of this close team, no one could appoint the summit group, and so, after considerable debate, they decided on a secret ballot. It must have been ludicrous to watch the tired men, on the narrow edge of life as they were, discussing and voting for two men to push even further. Yet vote they did, choosing Craig and Gilkey as the strongest of the group, to go to the top for all of them. Even as the storm increased, these two reviewed plans and supplies again and again. Ounces counted, yet they must not lack any essential. They hoped for clearing weather which might bring success.

But the storm continued. The wind seemed to increase with a malevolence almost personal in direction and fury. The tents thundered. Cold and lack of water dragged down their strength. Each morning and evening they talked over the small radio with Ata-Ullah, at base camp, who received weather forecasts specially made to them by Radio Pakistan. These had a monotonous pessimism: 'For the American K2 party: At 24,000 ft the weather will be cloudy with heavy snowfall. Winds will be westerly, blowing forty to forty-five knots, occasionally going to hurricane velocity.' It was warming to hear Ata's encouraging voice, but even this could not change the weather. Until it cleared they could not advance – and probably could not even retreat.

On 6 August came new trouble. Gilkey, apparently the strongest of the party, collapsed, and when Houston examined him the problem was terribly clear: a blood clot had formed in his left leg. . . . phlebitis, which at this altitude might be fatal. Gilkey had felt pain in his leg for several days, but blamed it on a pulled muscle. Now he could not stand and the risk of a piece of clot being carried to the lungs was serious. He would not be able to walk for many days, and before that they must get down or all die. Houston, with his medical training, knew this, but the others did not, and he felt he could not tell them everything. Perhaps even he did not at once grasp the hopelessness of the situation. Craig, Molenaar and Schoening were old hands at mountain rescue and were confident that their techniques could get the cripple down, but even their experience could not outweigh the problems of altitude, privation and storm, which would make doubly difficult the formidable climbing below. Few if any of the men appreciated how improbable was their survival; unbelievably they still looked upwards.

Their strategy had to be changed, however, and they now discussed taking Gilkey down, resting a few days at base camp, and returning to the attack. Incredible though it would have seemed to an observer looking over their shoulders, these wearied men contemplated without dismay carrying a helpless body down cliffs which were hard and dangerous enough to tax a healthy, unladen party. So strong had become the bonds between them that none thought of leaving him and saving themselves – it was not to be dreamed of, even though he would probably die of his illness. Failure did not occur to them; but the weather had to improve before they could even start.

On 7 August a dim sun burned through the scud above them, the wind slackened and it looked as though fair weather might be ahead. They decided to move and by ten o'clock were ready, taking with them only sleeping bags and precious film and diaries, for the camps below had been stocked in anticipation of such a forced retreat.

They even took a group picture, holding a paper flag – a composite of the flags of Pakistan, Britain, the United States and United Nations – which Molenaar had painted to leave on the summit. Houston held a great treasure – a stick of wood found in 1938 at the site of the high camp left by Luigi Amedeo, Duke of the Abruzzi, who had first tried K2 in 1909. He had taken this little fragment home and kept it for fifteen years hoping some day to leave it on the summit in tribute to the great explorer. The party was almost too tired to sit for this portrait, but the picture was taken; battered climbers, paper flag, wooden stick and all. Then, with Gilkey bundled in all his clothes, wrapped in the torn tent and bound securely with ropes, the party started out.

For a few yards they dragged their burden through snow up to their thighs. Then the slope grew steeper; three men were needed to hold back, two to pull, and two ahead to stamp out a trail. Steeper and steeper – five men to hold back and two ahead. Suddenly the leading men halted. Beneath the flour-fine snow was hard ice – ideal avalanche conditions. Hurriedly they consulted, almost in whispers. There was no need to talk long, for the slope was horribly dangerous and at any instant their motion or a loud noise might set thousands of tons of snow cascading down the cliffs. Their escape route was closed, for there was no way to cross or descend this great ice slope in such conditions. Carefully they began the fearful

Camp VIII during a lull in the storm on 2 August. The tent has blown down but the heaviest storms have not yet started.

work of hauling Gilkey up to camp. Down had been hard enough; the few hundred yards uphill took them many hours and nearly finished them all.

The day continued calm though an icy cloud lay over them, limiting visibility to a few yards. They could cook, however, and soon the stoves were melting snow, though it took an eternity to produce a few cups of water. In mid-afternoon two parties set out again: one started up – not in any hope of getting very high, but in a last act of defiance to show that their spirits were not broken. The other pair went to search for a possible route down a small rock rib which Schoening had noted on ascent. This rib would be safe from slides and it might lead to their old route near camp seven.

The high party came back after climbing only a few hundred yards. Much later the others returned, dead beat but happy. The rock rib was not too bad, they said; it steepened below the lowest point they had reached and might grow harder, but they believed it possible and safe to lower Gilkey to that point and probably farther. Once again escape might be possible, and they discussed plans with Ata-Ullah that night over the radio. 'Tomorrow, as early as possible, we start down, Ata; pray for us,' said Houston. 'Charlie, we here at base camp have been praying for you for many days,' came the reply.

But once again the weather changed their plans. The wind howled during the night and in the grey morning, snow and storm pinned them in their tents. It seemed impossible that wind could be so violent. The tents must surely tear to shreds. The noise was intolerable, and the banging of the fabric against their heads incessant. They could see nothing outside but a white tortured void. All through the day they lay in a semi-stupor, talking little, forcing themselves to swallow bits of chocolate, dried fruit, dried meat, or to suck on bits of ice. August 9 was the same – furious wind, fine-driven snow, bitter cold. Strength was ebbing, but spirits rose. So bad was their plight it could only get better, and they joked to Ata-Ullah on the radio, dictating letters for him to send home. Gilkey was worse, fearfully short of breath and coughing constantly; bits of clot had passed to both lungs, and his survival seemed a matter of hours.

The inner strength of the party was now their only hope. There was – fantastically – talk of the summit still: 'When we get Art down to base, we'll rest a few days and then come back up – the weather has to be settled fair by then.'

The morning of 10 August was calm, though ominously grey. The storm seemed to have decreased and they could see for a little distance. This would have to be the day; they must take a chance and start, for in a short time they would be too weak to move. This was their last chance because they would have no hope whatever of climbing back up if they could not get down. Houston called base camp: 'It's pretty desperate, Ata, but we can't wait. We're starting down now. We'll call you at three o'clock.'

Slowly they gathered their few essentials, once again wrapped Gilkey in the torn tent and trussed him securely. Houston gave him an injection to ease his pain and to spare him some consciousness of the hard hours ahead. At nine they started. No one of the party recalls the next few hours well. They lowered Gilkey down the rib, sometimes sliding him along the steep snow to one side, sometimes carrying him over jagged rocks. The wind returning in some force bit at them, and their faces caked with ice so that they were forced to remove their dark glasses, risking snow blindness. Hands and feet were frostbitten and numb. Foot by weary foot they moved down, without rest except while belay points were being found. It was too cold, and they were too tired to eat; there was nothing to drink. Slowly they inched down, safe at least from slides.

In the early afternoon they reached the little cliff that Schoening had seen. It was less than forty feet high and not specially difficult, though the rocks were loose and covered with rime, and powdery snow filled the crevices. Under ordinary conditions and in full strength they would have had little trouble there, but laden as they were, weary and numb to the bone, it was formidable. Molenaar and Schoening were ahead, carefully belayed by those above. Muffled voices were tattered by the wind: they were down, but what else were they shouting? Craig unroped and climbed part way down to relay signals. The others waited, then began to lower Gilkey. More unintelligible shouts came from below; they halted. After what seemed an eternity came a tug on the rope and they lowered again. Suddenly from Craig came a frantic shout: 'Hold tight, they're being hit by a slide.' They held.

Finally through the storm they could see all the figures bent to the slope – all were there, the snow slide had been small and the rope had held them. They began to lower Gilkey again. It took every ounce of strength and skill to hold him – once the rope almost slipped through their numb, gloved hands. Finally he came to rest on a small ledge, held by Schoening who established a firm belay by passing his rope twice about his ice axe shaft driven deeply into the snow behind a huge boulder. Molenaar then tied on to Gilkey's rope – an added precaution that was to save them all. Craig carefully worked his way over to the narrow ledge where camp seven had

The routes of ascent and descent to Camp VIII – sketch by Molenaar.

been and where they would have to spend the night.

Now the others – in two ropes of two – began the delicate descent. Schoening could see them dimly through the snow; Gilkey hung helplessly below him, held by the solid belay. Schoening saw one man safely down, another close behind him. Suddenly the second man fell, the first could not check him – both were sliding. A man on the second rope, close behind and slightly below, was hit, and almost instantly, one after another of the figures was plucked from the cliff and tumbled down the slope. Fascinated, Schoening watched them go. One man bounced over Gilkey's rope, entangling Molenaar and pulling him off too: now all but Schoening were falling. Then Schoening saw the rope below him tighten, and by a miracle of quickness and strength he held, allowing the rope to slide around his belay so that the full strain would not come at once, for he saw that all five men were held by the rope between him and Gilkey. He remembers watching the nylon stretch and grow thin, but it held, the grotesque figures came to rest; the fall was stopped.

In a few moments some of the sprawled figures began to move. Craig, unroped near camp seven, had watched horror-stricken, picturing himself the sole survivor. Schoening crouched over his belay, shouting to the others to get their weight off the rope. Bell was stunned, and had lost his glasses. Molenaar with a deep cut in his thigh and a cracked rib was in little better shape. Bates was shaken but unhurt, and Streather seemed untouched. Bates reached the unconscious Houston but could not rouse him. Close to his ear he said firmly, 'Charlie, if you ever want to see Dorcas and Penny again (his wife and daughter), get up and climb.' Like an automaton Houston stood and slowly scrambled up to the others. Schoening tied Gilkey to two ice axes driven deeply into the snow behind the life-saving boulder and helped to pitch the little tents on the narrow ledge chopped out of the ice where camp seven had been. Wind and snow hid everything as they worked. Gilkey, hanging inertly against the slope, still numb from the injection given earlier, was almost invisible though only a few hundred feet away, and the howling wind drowned all sounds. Craig, Bates and Streather crept back to take him food and comfort and the assurance that in a little while the whole party would be recovered enough for the tricky job of shifting him across the steep slope to camp.

The three peered through the storm. The slope looked different, as though swept clean by a giant broom. There was no trace of Gilkey, no ropes, no ice axes. Slowly they grasped what had happened – an avalanche had come down, carrying Gilkey to sudden certain death over the cliffs below. Stunned by this new tragedy they returned to the others. Even dulled as they were, the others realised what the fall meant to them. Gilkey, surely doomed by his illness, could never have been lowered over the cliffs below by men themselves injured and almost too weak to climb unburdened. They had taken seven hours to cover a few hundred feet – how could they have dared to hope to do thousands of steeper feet below? Gilkey was dead, lost in honourable circumstances, and the others, freed of their impossible burden, might now have a chance to live. But their safe descent would require all their skill and courage.

By a blessing the wind stopped and tea could be made all through the night. The tents were too crowded for sleep, and Houston, delirious, kept trying to cut a hole in the tent wall: 'We'll all die unless you get air in here,' he cried over and over again, rambling on about oxygen and high altitude. Schoening and Craig coughed incessantly. Molenaar could move only with great pain. At dawn the wind returned, though not in gale force. They had to move – camp seven was a certain avalanche trap and no supplies had been left there.

Bound by two climbing ropes whose security was more spiritual than real (in their numbed and weakened state no one could check a fall), they worked painfully down the smooth treacherous slabs which they regarded as the most dangerous portion of the route. Through swirling snow they came upon traces of the fall – shreds of sleeping bag and tent, tangles of rope, a broken

Molenaar's painting of the accident scene.

axe, blood, through which they had to climb. No one spoke of this, then or for years later. Each climbed carefully, guarding his companions; there were no slips. Like sick men walking in a dream they finally reached camp six – a haven of safety with food and fuel and two well-pitched and sheltered tents. They could make soup and tea and hot food, and they could really sleep. Strength returned; late on 13 August in falling snow they reached the top of House's Chimney.

This crack – about 150 ft high and four to eight feet wide – offers the only route up or down. Though it would be difficult enough at sea level, at 22,000 ft it is a formidable obstacle and each climbing group worried about being caught above it by storm. Now the whole party was caught, not only in storm, but in gathering darkness, and weak and injured as well. Should they try to get down that night or risk another night high on the mountain? To get down before dark was not possible, to climb in the dark would be hard, but to stay another night so high was unthinkable. They decided to go down. One by one, with deliberate speed, the climbers entered the crack, held and belayed by those above. Houston and Bates as leaders remained to the last; Houston insisting on belaying Bates down ahead of him. By then it was pitch dark, howling wind, and blowing snow.

Houston realised he could not climb down. He was still suffering from his fall and could not move his head without pain; there was no practical way to secure himself. Worst of all, the three ropes hanging in the chimneys were indistinguishable by feel in the dark: Two (left in 1938 and 1939) were rotten, and only the newest was safe. He dared not trust any of them but must climb down unaided. Many thoughts went through his head – the bitterness of defeat, the wasted work, and above all their friend's death. Now this hopeless descent, another defeat, another death. He decided to jump, ending the struggle without the risk of falling down the chimney and perhaps sweeping away those below. But he must have had some inner strength left, for he hesitated, unable to take this final step. Unintelligible shouts came from below. He knelt in the snow and whispered the Lord's Prayer.

Looking back over the years, Houston recalls those minutes with photographic detail, but he has no recollection of what followed. How he climbed down is a blank – his next memory is of being helped across the steep snow at the bottom of the chimney and down to the snug security of camp four where hot tea, food, and friends were waiting. To him as to them the safe descent was another miracle in their tragic epic.

Finally on 16 August they were down. At the foot of the ridge, Ata-Ullah met them, sick with worry, for they had lost their radio in the fall and his last word from them had come on the morning of the tenth when they started down.

Even the joys of safety – space to walk about in, comparative warmth, limitless water – could not completely heal the wounds of tragedy and defeat. On their first night at base camp they sat around the tape recorder while each man told his recollections of the terrible two weeks. Next day they built a cairn to Gilkey's memory and Bates read a short selection from the Bible – for him, but also for them all.

The return to civilisation was long and tedious, but it was literally a return to life, as each day brought new delights: grass and flowers, sweet smells, bird songs, warmth, and later fresh fruit, eggs, friendly villagers. After two weeks they reached Skardu, the airfield, and planes which took them home.

Opposite: Muztagh Tower from the south-east. The French route followed the ridge midway between the two 'ears' of the Tower.
Overleaf: The highest summit of the Muztagh Tower. Behind K2, about five miles away.

Chapter 3

The Background

'Plus ça change, plus c'est la même chose'

T.S.Blakeney

The early development of mountaineering has been the theme of many essays and much of it can be disregarded here. The main field of activity at first was in the Alps of Europe and the climbers of those days, from de Saussure in the 1780s down to the mid-nineteenth century, were actuated by a mixture of motives: scientific studies, such as glaciology; topographical enquiry – until mapping had got under way the tendency was to go for the highest peaks and forget the others; and sheer adventure – the challenge that mountains present to man's ability to know the Earth on which he dwells. Exploration in the widest sense was a notable feature of the nineteenth century – Arctic, Antarctic, Central Asia, Africa, Australia – and mountaineers could and did lend their specialised skills to reveal the mountainous areas that might be avoided by other explorers.

Any skilful pastime will develop its techniques; climbing was no exception, and many of the pioneers would today be judged to be technically incompetent. Periodical 'shots in the arm' were administered: by Whymper, when he triumphed over the Matterhorn in 1865; by Mummery in the 1880s; by the Zsigmondys and Purtscheller; and, in the early years of this century, by V.J.E. Ryan, Winthrop Young, Preuss, Pfann, and others. Concurrently with these developments in the Alps went the exploration of the remoter mountain ranges: North and South American, New Zealand, the Caucasus and, dominating all, the Karakoram-Himalaya.

Two undoubted influences made themselves

Opposite: View down the West Ridge of Muztagh Tower. The two tents of the Ridge Camp at 6,180 metres can just be seen.

North Face of Everest taken by William Unsoeld on the first ascent of the West Ridge in 1963. It was on this face that no less than six climbers without oxygen on early Everest expeditions reached 28,000 ft – a height that was not to be achieved again with oxygen for over a quarter of a century.

felt in the psychological sphere – the effects of the two World Wars of 1914–18 and 1939–45. The two decades between these wars saw a notable upsurge of mountaineering effort. The tradition of guided climbing was receding into the background; travel facilities were greatly enhanced; money was becoming more widely spread and enjoyed. Mountaineering ceased to be a preserve of a few and began to be popular and to attract press attention: it became news.

Salient features of these inter-war years may be summarised as: (i) Himalayan climbing, (ii) the Mont Blanc massif, (iii) 'north faces'. As regards (i), although Everest pre-occupied British Himalayan climbing rather a lot – seven expeditions – nevertheless it was not vain effort, for to reach over 28,000 ft by six climbers, without oxygen, was a noteworthy achievement, and the enterprises of Shipton, Tilman, Smythe and others during the thirties, with ascents of such peaks as Kamet, Nanda Devi, Chomolhari, Mana Peak and many more, showed that the draw of the highest peak of all was not prejudicial to a wider outlook on Himalayan adventure. At the same time, the Germans on Nanga Parbat and Kangchenjunga, the Americans on K2 and Minya Konka, and the Swiss, all showed how the attraction of the greatest of all mountain ranges was being felt. Prior to the outbreak of the Second World War, twenty-four peaks over 23,000 ft (7,000 metres and more) had been ascended, all in Asia, and nearly all in the Himalayas.

The second feature of inter-war climbing, the Mont Blanc range, was notable for the develop-

Central Pillar of Frêney.

Don Whillans on bivouac during first ascent of Central Pillar of Frêney.

ment of new standards in rock climbing technique – and in this the Dolomites were rivalling the Chamonix aiguilles – and the opening up of fresh routes on Mont Blanc itself. Prior to 1914, routes such as the Mer de Glace face of the Grépon, or the Ryan-Lochmatter route on the Plan, had been regarded as the last word in rock climbing difficulty; soon they were to become standard routes. Yet in the 1920s some aura of inaccessibility still clung to them, while as for Mont Blanc, excepting the Innominata route (first climbed in 1919), the trend had been to repeat the great ridge climbs of long standing (Old Brenva, Peuterey and Brouillard) until, in 1927 and 1928, Smythe and Graham Brown broke entirely fresh ground with routes from the Brenva glacier (Sentinelle Rouge and Route Major). The French climbers de Lepiney, de Ségogne, Lagarde, Pierre Allain, and others, and the great guide Armand Charlet, stimulated a notable renaissance in French mountaineering that had far-reaching effects. Italians like Comici and Cassin were doing the same in the Dolomites.

The third great feature of inter-war climbing was also developing – north faces. In strictness, not all the great faces climbed were truly 'north', and some were in the Mont Blanc massif already mentioned. But nothing caught the eye of the public more than the first ascent of the north face of the Matterhorn in 1931 by the Schmid brothers; not even the technically more formidable routes on the Eigerwand (1938) or north face of the Grandes Jorasses (1938) captured the imagination more than the Matter-

Overleaf: Mont Blanc and the Chamonix Aiguilles from Aiguille Verte.

horn had done; and Italian parties were soon to add direct routes up the eastern and southern faces.

Nor did the advent of the war in 1939 entirely stop the development of technique in climbing. The Swiss, and some French and Italians, managed to continue mountaineering – for example, Gervasutti, one of the greatest rock-climbers; Terray, Lachenel and Rébuffat. Terray, indeed, in his well-known book, goes so far as to date the revival of French mountaineering to the years of the Second World War, but this is unjust to earlier climbers.

In the two decades since the Second World War ended, there has been an immense expansion, amounting almost to a revolution. In the Alps the feature most in evidence has been the abundant use of pitons to overcome obstacles impossible to 'free' climbing. Pitons were not new, but they had been sparingly used hitherto; in 1935, for example, Allain and Leininger's climb of the Petit Dru by the north face had made but little use of them. Seventeen years later, the west face of the Petit Dru was ascended by Magnone's party by means of lavish use of these aids, and indeed this climb might almost be taken as the most significant event (as regards rock technique) since the war, as it inaugurated a fashion that has caught on abundantly all over the Alps as well as in North America (for instance, in the Yosemite Valley).

But mountaineering is more than mere technique, and the opening up of the Himalayas may fairly be regarded as the greatest single feature in post-war climbing, with a parallel opening up of the Andes ranking near after it. As already noted, two dozen peaks over 7,000 metres in height had been climbed up to 1939, and as the beginnings of high climbing in the Himalaya had begun at least by 1883 (W. W. Graham's expedition), these twenty-four peaks represent the 'bag' in over half a century (although, of course, numerous peaks under 7,000 metres had also been ascended – in 1935 alone, Shipton's party round Everest accounted for a total of twenty-two peaks, including three over 23,000 ft). In ten years, 1947–57, over thirty more, above 7,000 metres, were accounted for, and during the next decade, 1957–67, all the remaining giants of 8,000 metres and up had been climbed, to say nothing of some fifty between 7,000 and 8,000 metres. Countries involved have included Great Britain, Austria, France, Switzerland, Germany, Italy, Poland, New Zealand, America, Japan, India, and China.

At slightly lower altitudes, much valuable exploration and mapping has been done, even in obscure areas such as Bhutan. One very striking feature in these post-war years has been the admission of foreigners to Nepal to an extent unimaginable before 1939. By contrast, Tibet, since 1950, is more closed than ever before, and indeed political frontier troubles have in late years severely restricted access to the Karakoram and Himalayas alike.

American and Canadian climbers have on their doorstep a huge field for exploration in Alaska, the Yukon and the Coast Range, and since the war they have cleaned up the virgin peaks in these areas remarkably, and an intensive era of alternative routes has begun. Other countries have, in recent years, introduced themselves to these same regions, but in the main it is American enterprise that has handled the exploration.

In the Andes, the loftiest peaks had mostly been climbed before 1939, but since the war there has been much activity among these

On the Rochfort Arête.

phenomenally photogenic mountains. Peru, more than any other country, has been the scene of mountaineering enterprise, but Colombia, Ecuador and Bolivia have also been explored, and a welcome feature has been the work of University parties in surveying and mapping the numerous ranges comprised under the name 'Andes'. Farther south, in Patagonia, the very severe rock peaks of FitzRoy and the Cordillera Paine have attracted climbing parties from more than one country, while Tilman, and still more Shipton, to say nothing of Chilean and Argentinean adventurers, have penetrated the Patagonian ice-cap and the mountains in the far south in Tierra del Fuego.

At the extremes of the Arctic and the Antarctic, mountain exploration and climbing has been a feature of the post-war era, especially in the first-named region. Air transport now places Greenland within the range of a relatively brief holiday from Europe, and the Stauning Alps have been penetrated and mapped by numerous parties. Northern or West Greenland, and the Canadian Archipelago, are more inaccessible, but have yielded their secrets to determined parties, while islands like Iceland and Spitsbergen are virtually exhausted for the mountaineer intent on novelty. The remoteness of Antarctica has militated against exploitation, but the I.G.Y. gave an impetus to exploration, which must continue so long as the bases are maintained that give parties something of a flying start in these vast wastes of snow and ice. The Americans have taken the lead in this, but New Zealand has also done good work, and it may be regarded as certain that, provided finances do not fail, the opening up of these frigid regions will continue.

It may well be asked how is it that, in the twenty-odd years since the last war ended, there has been so much triumph on mountains which not long before either had repelled all attempts to climb them or were not even attempted? It seems possible to discern four main strands of influence that have produced these results, without counting public interest as exemplified in the press.

Firstly, following both wars, there has been a break-away from the traditional leading strings of classical mountaineering. Guided climbing became the exception and in consequence the amateur, obliged or determined to rely on himself, became more expert. The distinction, indeed, between guide and amateur has become blurred. Among Continentals, with their mountains near at hand, this movement has been in existence for quite a long time; among the English it became marked as the young climber, accustomed to the severe, if short, climbs provided by his own hills, went abroad far more expertly trained than had been the case even twenty or thirty years earlier.

Secondly, there developed a new outlook about difficulties and dangers. Earlier generations of climbers might rule out automatically certain climbs as impossible; readers of books by such writers as Terray or Rébuffat will know that 'impossible' is a word that hardly exists for them today, thanks to modern climbing developments, especially piton technique. And it stands to reason that if a man has, by his own assiduous practice and by virtue of specialised equipment, become capable of riskier and more formidable climbs than his predecessors could undertake, he will tend to attempt such climbs. Between the wars a new mental outlook was in growth; if one was prepared to risk life more readily than in the past, one could be certain of making climbs that an earlier generation would have ruled out. That lives might be lost in the process was true (and regrettable), but the new climbs were made, none the less.

It is impossible to disregard the fact that earlier climbers regarded loss of life more seriously than we do today; no doubt the wars have to take some responsibility for this change of outlook. Frank Smythe, writing in 1939 of the Matterhorn disaster of 1865, says,

> It is impossible not to reflect that human life was more precious in 1865 than it is in 1939. Nowadays an accident, whether in mountaineering or in one or other of the death dealing forms of locomotion, is passed by almost without comment and soon forgotten, but in 1865 life was a sacred thing, due possibly to a stronger religious background than today.

It is difficult to recapture the extent of lamentation that arose even so late as the 1930s over the death of J. D. Hoyland on Mont Blanc.

Thirdly, equipment has made great strides, not merely in terms of artificial aids, such as pitons, etriers, and the like, but in down clothing, sleeping bags, boots, ropes, etc. Given these improvements to physical well-being on the mountain, a climber today can make climbs, and especially climbs involving bivouacs, that would have been unjustifiable for earlier generations. Along with equipment developed better knowledge of many factors in climbing; the success on Everest in 1953 owed a debt not only to preceding expeditions to the mountain, but also to a clearer understanding of physiological consequences of high altitude climbing, with resultant changes in the methods of dealing with dehydration and oxygen deficiency. Add improved guide books, maps and information generally, and the mountaineer of today must admit that he is well placed, compared with his predecessor.

Fourthly, there is the psychological breakthrough that results from knowing that a particular feat of climbing (or its near equivalent) has been done. Just as the first breaking of the four-minute mile was quickly followed by other instances of it, at increasing speeds, so the aura of impossibility in mountains has broken down. This change in mental approach is hard to define, but it cannot be doubted that the mystique of climbing as understood by our ancestors has largely disappeared.

It has not been all gain. The basic change has been a shift of interest away from the mountain to the climber.

> It is part of the human tragedy of our destiny as beings in isolation and in egoism, that the more we become aware and the further we progress in perfecting our skills and executing our ideas, the less we can continue to derive from original inspiration.

Opposite: Géant from Niche des Amis on Mer de Glace face of Grépon.

Matterhorn, North Face disappears in cloud on the right.

So said Geoffrey Young in 1956 and it was a theme he had expressed earlier and was to express later. Something that held mountaineers together in the past is in danger of being lost, if the wider, more humane approach to mountaineering is at first diluted, and eventually swamped, by the floodwaters of technique and personal expertise. Scarcely less ominous has been the substitution of national prestige for healthy mountaineering ambition. Whilst nationalist rivalry had not been absent in early days, it was only in the inter-war period that mountaineering achievement came to be regarded as a proper means of enhancing a nation's fame.

Considered as a sport, mountaineering has changed in character, and the change is likely to continue, now that commercialism has set its hand upon it. So long as mountain exploration continues however (and there is scope enough), something of the old-time sense of mystery and romance can be felt, though some loss must be experienced as, in the glare of modern times, 'a climb becomes less a venture into the unknown than the performance of a more or less prescribed exercise'. Fashions, however, change between generations, and the outlook of individuals varies with the passage of years. Mountains provide a wide range of experiences and no matter how often a peak, or a route, may have been climbed by others, to the individual viewing it for the first time it is always in some measure new. Pioneering in the literal sense may become increasingly rare, but those who seek for enjoyment among mountains can always find it.

Bonington leads Boysen on first ascent of Medlar, Ravens Crag.

Chapter 4

The Nurseries

Today the world boasts a hundred training grounds but the Lakes, North Wales and Scotland are so steeped in the history, lore and development of mountaineering, and lie so close to the hearts of so many great mountaineers, that they claim special mention. The Yosemite Valley, although a nursery in the sense that it is a relatively small district, easily reached, nevertheless yields some of the most formidable artificial climbing in the world

THE LAKES *A.H.Griffin*

Rock climbing in Britain began in the late summer of 1882 when W. P. Haskett Smith, a twenty-three year old university man with a taste for adventure, sought out and climbed several damp, moss-filled gullies cleaving the crags of Great End, Bowfell, Pavey Ark and Gimmer Crag in the English Lake District. And in the same year he reached the top of Pillar Rock by new routes up the short, steep side out of Jordan Gap. Pillar Rock had been climbed by a shepherd nearly sixty years before; the awkward corner of Broad Stand on Scafell had been surmounted even earlier and two or three isolated routes had been made up the sides of the crags, but this batch of lone ascents by young Haskett Smith really marked the beginning of the sport. For the first time the idea of climbing rocks for the fun of the thing, instead of to reach the top of a mountain or peak, was born.

The crags of Lakeland consist, for the most part, of cliffs of clean volcanic rock, ranging from fifty feet outcrops to precipices towering five hundred feet or more. The pioneers who followed Haskett Smith first climbed the gullies, chimneys and cracks that rive these crags and then ventured out on to the ridges and steep walls in between where the exposure was greater. They climbed in heavily nailed shepherds' boots – or in socks when the holds became slippery or sloping – and, later, in rubber plimsolls, until moulded rubber soles became almost universal. Wasdale Head, the tiny hamlet between the Scafell crags and the airy ridges of Great Gable, became their Mecca, and the old inn where the legendary Will

Opposite: The climbers in the centre are in Gimmer Crack, the figure on the right skyline is on Kipling Groove.

Black Crag in the little valley of Troutdale; a climb of great charm.

Ritson had entertained the nineteenth-century fellwalkers, their first headquarters.

But since these days of Norfolk-jacketed men of leisure, Lakeland climbing has undergone tremendous changes. Siegfried Herford's lead in 1914 of Central Buttress on Scafell, with its overhanging Flake Crack, marked the first big advance; Kelly, Bower and others led the post-war era, and Birkett and Dolphin were among the forerunners of the present modern school, where the challenge of smooth, vertical rock is welcomed. Most of today's younger climbers operate from huts scattered through all the main valleys and artificial climbing has at last been accepted. In the early days the rocks had been sacrosanct. The early climbers used their ice-axes for jammed holds in summer time as a matter of course, but

Eliminate A, Dhow Crag.

when Collie hacked out his famous step in the rock wall of Moss Ghyll he did so almost with shame and had to face widespread criticism. Pitons were first used on Lake District crags purely as emergency belays and when Linnell hammered one, as direct aid, into Overhanging Wall on Scafell's east buttress in 1933 he was striking a new defiant note. Today, however, pitons are in regular use on many of the hardest routes – half the climbs in the extremely severe section of the latest Langdale guide normally involve their use – although purely artificial routes are still comparatively rare.

Undoubtedly, the principal attraction of Lakeland climbing lies in the multiplicity of free climbing routes of all degrees of severity. Fifty years ago there were about 170 rock climbs in the Lake District; today there are well over a thousand and the hardest of them attain a technical standard hardly exceeded anywhere in Europe. Climbers can learn their craft here on clean unshattered rock and progress, as many of them do, to the hardest rock routes in the Alps. Or they can rest content with the challenge of magnificent natural lines up great cliffs where the pioneers of the sport first scratched their way and, if they are young and daring, still find new routes through the overhangs or across near-holdless walls. The Lake District crags will always be a fine training ground but, to happy thousands, they are also an end in themselves. This is where it all began, and the joys of stepping neatly up perfect rock to some bilberry-decked ledge, and the evening stroll down through the bracken for a drink in a cool, shadowed room in the valley, are still among the best things in life for thousands of lovers of beauty and adventure.

Hiereth, Dove Crag, one of the hardest routes in the Lakes.

Snowdon from Capel Curig.

NORTH WALES *E.C.Pyatt*

It would be a mistake to regard climbing in North Wales solely as practice for Alpine mountaineering. This view was expressed more than fifty years ago by the pioneer climber, J. M. Archer Thomson –

> The difference between Welsh and Alpine climbing is not a difference of magnitude only but of essential quality, and dissimilarity of method has been accentuated by specialisation.

His view that 'British climbing is not undeveloped Alpinism but diverse' is even more obviously true today.

The hill groups mostly fall within the 800 square miles of the Snowdonia National Park. On a world scale these are small mountains, the highest, Snowdon, only 3,560 ft, but even though there is no peak which cannot be reached by walking alone they mean a great deal to British climbers. The climbing is on crag faces, from 100 to 500 ft high, mostly on mountainsides, though in a few cases (notably Tryfan and Lliwedd) the crags give on to the mountain top. Unlike the Lake District, where the heart of the mountains is not penetrated by roads, the Snowdonian mountains are dissected by road passes which give ready access to the climbing crags.

Nowadays climbers in Wales can be divided into two groups with widely diverging outlooks. Those of the traditional school, stemming from Archer Thomson, are on the whole less competent technically. They climb for personal satisfaction, are non-competitive and never deliberately court a fall. Their crags are the faces of Tryfan, Cwm Idwal, Lliwedd and so on, and they sometimes continue to the top of the mountain when

Opposite: Lliwedd.

their rock climb is done. The modern school, highly competent technically, and fiercely competitive, has arisen during the last fifteen years, helped on by the advent of nylon rope, the increased use of artificial aids and the acceptance of falling off, when adequately safeguarded, as the price of finding out how. The 'moderns' climb in the Llanberis Pass, on Clogwyn Du'r Arddu, and indeed on all the steepest crags; unsound rock and bad conditions do not worry them and they seldom visit a Welsh mountain top. Abroad, their achievements have placed them in the forefront of world mountaineering.

New climbs in Wales no longer follow lines of weakness; instead the climber traces a tenuous line of fortuitously occurring holds with occasional cracks for pitons. While such lines can be multiplied by the few for the few, what will be the broad direction of future progress? There are two interesting modern developments. The first has taken climbers to the plains by Tremadoc, where a series of 200 ft rock walls gives what is really large scale outcrop climbing. The second is the recent exploration of sea cliffs in Anglesey. Both these are a stage removed from mountaineering, treating the technical problems of climbing as an end in themselves.

Meanwhile the mountains, unspoilt as yet by hydro-electric schemes, television masts, military training or water supply, remain much the same. They are more crowded now, yet it should still be possible by selection of time and place to find here, as did the poet of Pen y Pass, 'much comfort . . . and a great easing of the heart'.

Left: Cliff climb, Anglesey.
Opposite: Pincushion, Tremadoc.

The nurseries

Opposite: Climbers on Clogwyn Y Grochan.

Dinas Mot.

Cairn.

SCOTLAND *T.W.Patey*

There is potentially more climbing in Scotland than in either England or Wales but disproportionately fewer climbers. So far, the supply of new routes has proved sufficient to meet any demands, and in the far north-west you may today find vast crags of 'Cloggy' dimensions which still preserve their secrets for a future generation.

Because of their proximity to the big cities, Glen Coe and, to a lesser extent, the Cobbler, have usually set a trend in Scottish rock climbing. Glen Coe is the only Scottish climbing ground where new developments have consistently matched those in the south. Here during the first post-war decade, the partisans of the Creag Dhu Club, led by Cunningham, Bill Smith and MacInnes, set the pace for future exploration. Their philosophy and route conception owed little to pre-war influence, and their contributions – bold exacting climbs on exposed faces – were a complete antithesis of the confined gully routes of the thirties. The athletic prowess of individual Creag Dhu members is almost legendary. Several won the Scottish 'Kandahar' and when organised skiing reached Scotland in the late fifties many migrated to Speyside to become professional ski instructors. This left the field open for a second wave of Edinburgh 'hard men', including the members of the Squirrels Mountaineering Club – currently the most active group in the country. Two of the original Creag Dhu veterans are still to the fore – John Cunningham, the most stylish climber Scotland has produced, and Hamish MacInnes, mountain rescue expert and master craftsman, with a long

Opposite: The party who made the first complete winter traverse of the main Cuillin Ridge – Robertson with helmet, Crabbe and standing, Patey. Hamish MacInnes took the picture. The expedition took two days.

Right: Crack of Dawn on the East Face of Sgurr Mhic Coinnich, Skye first ascended by W. D. Brooker in 1951.

and colourful catalogue of new routes to his credit. In 1953 this pair visited Pumori in Nepal, for a total outlay of £30, which included the wages of one porter. (He was a humane man who presented his sahibs with a knife, fork and spoon on leaving – they had been reduced to using pitons.)

It was in the Cairngorms and Lochnagar area, once an undisputed province of the hill walker, that one of the most significant post-war trends had its earliest origins. This area saw the emergence of the modern school of Scottish ice climbing – a definitive brand of mountaineering with its own individualised techniques, and the philosophy that all summer routes are potential winter routes, requiring only extra effort and determination. The short ice-axe for one-handed cutting, became indispensable – ice pitons and artificial ice techniques played little or no part. Scotland's traditional image as a winter training ground for the Alps now requires to be remoulded, for the most experienced Alpinist would need time to adjust to Scottish ice techniques which are now as highly developed as any in Europe.

The small nucleus of Aberdeen climbers who initiated this movement discovered over fifty new winter routes in the Cairngorms between 1950 and 1956. They also demonstrated that Cairngorm granite, despite an evil reputation, could provide routes on its exposed vertical faces to rival those of Arran – another granite reserve which has recently been rediscovered. Cairngorm routes multiplied until they eventually exceeded Glen Coe and Skye but the main assets of the area are the consistent snow conditions which provide ice-climbing from December to May.

The early Scottish winter pioneers included MacInnes in Glen Coe (Raven's Gully 1953), and Brooker, Taylor, Patey and Nicol in the

Opposite: A vintage snow climb – the Crowberry Gully on the Buachaille. Such Alpine-style ascents have little in common with modern Scottish winter face routes which might be more properly described as iced-up rock climbs.

Etive Slabs which yield some twenty routes of the top Scottish grading – very severe. John Cunningham leading his own route Hammer.

Cairngorms. In 1957 the two last-named joined forces with MacInnes to complete the long awaited first winter ascent of Zero Gully, so extending the winter campaign to Ben Nevis and stimulating a spate of exploration.

The winter ascent of Parallel Gully B on Lochnagar by J. R. Marshall in 1957 ended the dominance of the Aberdeen school. Marshall, probably the most gifted ice climber of his day, was the first of a royal line of Edinburgh climbers who dictated subsequent trends in Scottish mountaineering – Robin Smith (whose meteoric career ended tragically in the Pamirs), Dougal Haston (a member of the international team which accounted for the winter Direttissima on the Eiger), Dave Bathgate and Brian Robertson.

After 1957 the winter spotlight moved to Ben Nevis and the remote Coire Ardair of Creag Meaghaidh. On the Ben, Clough led the first winter ascent of Point Five Gully (in five days!) and Marshall and Robin Smith repeated the route in six hours, also adding the more formidable 'Winter Direttissima' of the Orion Face.

It is probably true to say that Scottish ice climbing in the 1950–60 decade advanced more rapidly in scope and technique than rock climbing exploration had done over a twenty-five year period.

In the rock climbing field most of the noteworthy 'plums' fell to local patriots but there were exceptions. Most remarkable were Whillans' two great classics on the Carn Dearg buttress – Sassenach and Centurion – which shattered existing psychological barriers.

Opposite: Climber on the last pitch of Trapeze on the West Face of Aonach Dubh.

Left: Crucible of modern Scottish ice climbing – the north-eastern Corrie of Lochnagar.
Below: Patey leading Jerry Smith on the first winter ascent of Parallel Buttress, Lochnagar, a climb complicated by deep powder snow lying on frozen vegetation.
Bottom: J. R. Marshall on the first winter ascent of Parallel Gully 'B', Lochnagar.

Opposite: Mechanised climbing on the Cobbler.

Bullroar, Ben Nevis – a rising traverse across the Carn Dearg Buttress which yields 1,000 ft of v.s. climbing.

Eastern Traverse on Tower Ridge, Ben Nevis.

In the north-west, exploration has been sporadic although a miniature gold rush ensues each time a new crag is discovered. Ben Lair (1951), Applecross (1952–3), Coire Mhic Fhearchair (intermittent), Foinaven (1966–7) – each for a time was the focus of intense exploration. The great 800-ft crag of Carn Mor (1956–7) was perhaps the most important find, yielding many long routes on magnificent Lewisian gneiss.

Elsewhere there has been considerable activity on valley crags which have been previously overlooked, such as the Etive Slabs and Creag Dubh of Newtonmore. A rekindling of enthusiasm for coast climbing is another symptom of the times.

By traditionally accepted standards of route discrimination, popular 'stamping-grounds' like the Rannoch Wall and the Cobbler are now approaching saturation point and even on less frequented crags 'new routes for old men' are harder to come by. For the habituees of Slime Wall however, there are no prospects of a stalemate. On nearly every Scottish mountain, horizons have broadened with the introduction of new skills and new techniques.

There is 'an epic quality', described by Bill Murray, which characterises the great Scottish routes, and in a wider sense distinguishes mountaineering from crag climbing. This 'epic quality' still prevails, and it will not diminish in this generation, nor yet in the next. Exploration is still the corner-stone of Scottish mountaineering.

Opposite: Douglas Scott captures the massive magnificence of the north-east buttress of Ben Nevis – a picture taken during the first winter ascent of Zero Gully. The three members of the party can just be made out above the right of the two-eared snow slope, centre.

Dave Bathgate on the long traverse on the second pitch of Carnivore, Creag a Bhancair.

Opposite: The first ascent of the 250 ft Ram's Head Buttress of Cobbler was accomplished in July 1967 by Amatt and Baillie in two one-day sorties, a rope being left in position overnight. Here Amatt swings well clear of the rock in an attempt to pass the lip of the overhang.
Overleaf: The summit ridge of Bidean nam Bian.

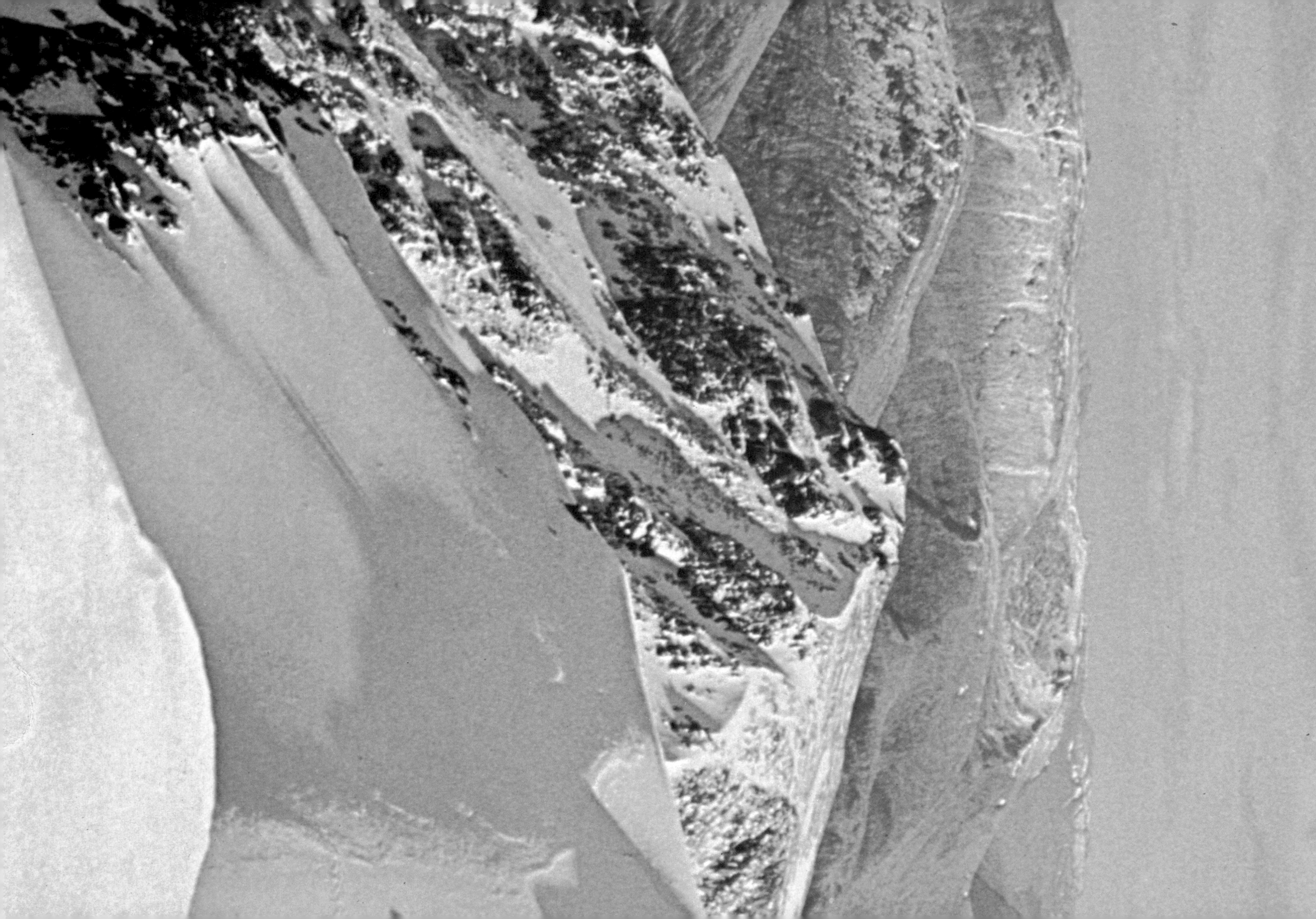

Charles Pratt on the West Buttress of El Capitan.

YOSEMITE *Royal Robbins*

Yosemite Valley is seven miles long, one mile wide, and 3,000 ft deep. The west entrance is guarded by the 3,000 ft bulk of El Capitan, while the noble mass of Half Dome, with its 2,000 ft north-west face, dominates the east end. Between them lies a myriad of great and small rocks, 1,000 ft waterfalls, verdant meadows, stately pines and a lovely placid river. It is very beautiful and highly accessible, a combination which has often proven disastrous to the beauty spots on this Earth. I doubt if there has ever existed a place more serene than Yosemite in its pristine state. That state is long past, but occasionally, in the off-season, one can perceive how it must have been.

The climbers in Yosemite don't climb to avoid the crowds, but the population pressures certainly add to their desire to escape to the vertical world above.

The Valley climbers are intense individuals. They must be, for the demands of climbing there are such that one cannot be 'happy-go-lucky' and succeed. Yosemite is like Clogwyn Du'r Arduu, in having almost no easy routes. Yet it is far bigger than 'Cloggy' and all the other areas in North Wales put together. (A glance in the Yosemite Guide will illustrate this.) Although there are over three hundred routes, only about sixty are in the first seven divisions of an eleven division classification system.

So we see that Yosemite can hardly be truly considered a 'nursery', as it is so unsuitable for novices. Climbers from all over the United States train in their own areas and train hard

Opposite: Richard Calderwood prussiking on the first ascent of the South Buttress of El Capitan.

Overleaf: Yosemite Valley – Royal Arches and Half Dome in the clouds.

before coming to the Valley. However, as Yvon Chouinard has pointed out, Yosemite can be considered a training ground in the sense of preparing climbers to face very difficult technical problems in the high mountains. But climbers do not yet come to the Valley to *train*. They come to face the biggest rock-climbing challenges in North America.

The competitive spirit in Yosemite is another element which adds to the tenseness of the climbers there. They form a small community in Camp 4, and almost everything that is done on the walls is known about and naturally discussed. This discussion leads to comparisons and so to a desire to 'do better'. Normally this competitive spirit is good-natured and healthy; sometimes it is mean-spirited and malicious; many climbers are hardly affected by it. But let the visitor beware of falling into the hands of a young 'hot-shot', eager for attention. Many unsuspecting victims have found themselves struggling desperately half-way up a climb that calls for a technique they have never developed.

Yosemite rock-climbing is a distinctive branch of mountaineering, played in its own special way with its own special rules. There are two main divisions in the way it is played; free-climbing and artificial. In Europe, 'artificial' climbing is when one uses a short rope ladder attached to a piton for progress. In Yosemite, *any* use of a piton or sling for physical support, with or without a rope ladder, is 'artificial' and hence 'cheating' on a free climb. On the other hand, unlike Great Britain, one may use an infinite

Charles Raymond leading Moby Dick, a practice climb at the base of El Capitan.

Royal Robbins.

El Capitan.

Looking down the Nose of El Capitan from 2,500 ft level. The triangular ledge in the foreground is 'Camp 6'.

Jim Baldwin on the Dihedral Wall, El Capitan.

Opposite: The pendulum to Stoveleg Crack. Dick McCracken and Gary Colliver on the nose of El Capitan.

Tom Frost 2,200 ft up the South Buttress of El Capitan.

Robbins on difficult friction climbing on the Salathé Wall.

number of pitons for protection and still call it 'free climbing'.

Yosemite, with its good weather and long vertical crack systems, is the perfect area for developing the technique of artificial climbing to its limits. There now exists what could properly be termed the 'Yosemite School of Artificial Climbing'. Fathered by John Salathé, shortly after the Second World War, this 'School' has its own methods, equipment, and philosophy. While the methods and philosophy have hardly been accepted everywhere, the equipment is widely regarded as the finest in the world.

However, 'free-climbing' intrigues valley climbers more than 'artificial', for they feel that managing a route without any aids, except the psychological ones of pitons for protection, is a more challenging game than artificial. Indeed, free-climbing dominates the scene on all the shorter climbs in Yosemite. In recent years much attention has been devoted to doing routes all free, and this has led to some quite astounding successes.

Certain free-climbing problems exist in Yosemite which are not encountered elsewhere, at least not to such a degree. To begin with, the rock tends to be smooth and the holds rounded. Good horizontal ledges are rare and 'buckets' even more rare. Yosemite walls are the antitheses of the great limestone faces in the Dolomites with their many horizontal fractures and holds. The smoothness of the rock usually prevents climbing the walls except by using vertical cracks and weaknesses. These cracks are often of a nature

Opposite: The Salathé Wall of El Capitan, bordered by the West and South Buttresses.

Chuck Pratt belaying in slings as Tom Frost follows his lead on the first ascent of the overhanging Headwall.

characteristic of Yosemite: four to eight inches wide, smooth, overhanging, and flared. Some of the hardest crack problems in North America are found along the base of El Capitan and in the canyon just below Yosemite Valley. A hint of their nature is given by some of their names: 'Crack of Doom', 'Crack of Despair', 'Twilight Zone'. These routes are similar to the 'Fissure Brown' in Chamonix and to the 'Right Hand Eliminate' at Kirber in England, but much longer.

Besides crack climbing, the other major area of free-climbing challenge in Yosemite is face climbing on low angle slabs. This activity is carried to its fullest expression on the 1,000 ft long Glacier Point Apron. Here footwork and grace are far more important than strength. The climbing is extremely difficult and some bold leads have been made. However, most of the really difficult climbing is protected with pitons or with bolts placed in holes drilled into the smooth granite. While some of the routes go all the way up the Apron, most terminate at obscure ledges whimsically called 'pinnacles'.

The only extensive face climbing on *steep rock* in the valley is found on middle and higher Cathedral Rocks. Some long, difficult, and sustained routes, with pitons for protection only, have been done here. One of them is almost 1,500 ft long and hard all the way.

But the real meat of Yosemite climbing, the aspect which is gaining it a world-wide reputation, is the 'big wall climbing'. Getting up a big face in Yosemite usually requires competence in

The Three Cathedral Rocks. The North-East Face of Middle Cathedral Rock with its great face climbs is in the centre.

Belay position on Friction Slabs on Salathé Wall.

both artificial and free techniques, plus endurance and speed.

The most popular big wall climbs in Yosemite are the north face of Sentinel Rock and the north-west face of Half Dome. But there are many others; pre-eminent among them, looming a thousand feet above its rivals, is El Capitan. There are now seven 'big' routes on El Capitan. The first was the south buttress, climbed in 1958, and repeated twelve times by the end of 1967. Climbing time on this, the least difficult route, ranges from three to seven days. The hardest route is the south-east face, or North America Wall. This somewhat shorter climb (2,400 ft) was first ascended in a ten-day effort in 1964. It has not been repeated.

But the best route on El Capitan, and perhaps

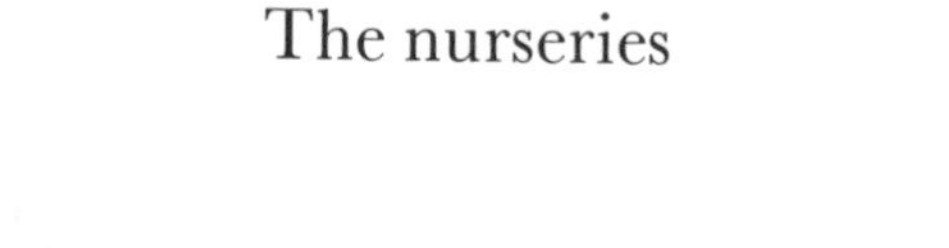

North-west Face of Half Dome. Standard route on left, direct on right.

Key:

A – Crescent Crack
B – Flake Ledge (second Bivouac)
C – First Terrace
D – Second Terrace
E – Last Terrace
F – The Zig-Zags
G – Thank God Ledge.

Opposite: North Face of Sentinel Rock on which there are seven rou

Richard McCracken approaching the summit overhangs on the North-West Face of Half Dome.

the finest rock-climb in the world, is the Salathé Wall, first done in 1961. The Salathé Wall achieves a special distinction through a superb combination of elements. (I doubt if anywhere else there is such a happy combination of beauty, variety, difficulty, and excellent rock on a great rock wall.) Four ascents have been made.

Yosemite climbing is a very modern phenomenon. Although the Cathedral Spires were climbed with pitons before the Second World War, the first big wall route, the Lost Arrow Chimney, was not opened up until 1947; and the second, the north wall of Sentinel, was first done in 1950. For years Yosemite climbers went quietly about their business, pushing the standards higher and higher and developing new techniques and equipment. Dismissed as acrobats, they were largely ignored until 1964, when the *American Alpine Journal* devoted its first four articles to Yosemite climbing. Since then the valley has gained a wide respect, and more and more foreign climbers, especially British, are going there. But I advise visitors not to go in the summer, when the heat and crowds are dreadful. Autumn is a good time, but spring is best, for then the waterfalls are roaring in their full splendour, the meadows are green, the days long, and the temperatures mild. In spring the incomparable valley dons her best clothes and most gracious smile, to greet the climbers who come fired with early season energy, ambition, and enthusiasm to enjoy themselves and test themselves on Yosemite's appealing and appalling walls.

Opposite: Half Dome with Tenaya Canyon on left.

Overleaf: Summer storm in Yosemite.

An 1897 group, left to right: George Abraham, O. G. Jones, N. J. Williams, C. Fox and Ashley Abraham.

GUIDED AND GUIDELESS CLIMBING *C. Douglas Milner*

'Persons who ascend mountains are known as mountaineers: those who descend them are known as survivors: professional survivors are known as guides.' That extract from an American book on mountains, of fifty years ago, summarises the general opinion prevailing before the modern age of mountaineering.

The Alpine Club was formed in 1857 and for half a century – if no more – was the principal fount of wisdom and knowledge in the mountain world. On the subject of guides it spoke with authority after Crauford Grove's paper read on 13 June 1870, in the course of which Grove made the perfectly sensible comment that 'making excursions without guides is no doubt a bolder and harder thing than making them with guides, but mountaineering, however bold and hardy or not, *is after all a sport and not a duty*'. The meeting decided that 'neglect to take guides on difficult expeditions, and especially the neglect to take them when the party is not exclusively composed of practised mountaineers, is totally unjustifiable, and calculated to produce the most lamentable results'. Arnold Lunn has written of this resolution as 'deplorable' but I cannot agree with him. It was right and necessary in that day and age, when no rock-climbing had been developed in Britain, when few alpine huts and no bivouac shelters had been built and when equipment was primitive.

It had been only a few years since the formation of the first continental alpine associations, those of the Swiss and the Austrians, with the express objects of erecting night stations in

Guided and guideless climbing

higher regions, and the *selection and education of able guides*. Guides' societies had already come into existence, notably that of Chamonix, which dated from 1821, and later that of Zermatt. Elsewhere, guides were a miscellaneous collection of men, many merely valley peasants accustomed to carrying heavy weights (a prime quality when heavy tents, firewood and ladders were taken), others perhaps chamois hunters, frontier smugglers, old soldiers from the mountain battlefields of Italy, France or Austria; as well as a few who have used their natural talents to become real mountaineers, though even they spent much of their time on the mountain hacking a staircase in hard snow or ice.

The contrast between the Chamonix guides and those of most other alpine districts became very marked. The former were very largely made up of mere muleteers, or guides for simple tours of the Mer de Glace, and the walk up Mont Blanc. The restrictive rules of the society, imposed by the Sardinian Government, were a constant source of complaint by the Alpine Club, particularly as skills and ambitions developed, for each man had to be engaged in turn regardless of his capacity. It was no wonder that the better climbers brought their own Valais or Oberland men with them, and in the latter half of the century there were few élite guides who did not come from those parts of Switzerland.

In that country, in Austria, also in Italy and in Norway, the large and growing alpine or tourist associations encouraged and controlled the corps of guides, laying down basic rules of conduct, establishing tariffs, and later on establishing systems of insurance so that the hardships of an accident, in their effect upon a guide's family, were to that extent reduced.

The system of guided climbing is too easily condemned today. Mountaineering demands time and money. Men of the Victorian age and the present day alike, who have some responsibilities in a wider world, who lack time but have adequate money, rightly try to buy something of the former with the latter. If you have, as had the early pioneers, the benefit of a long vacation (in Forbes' day, from a Scottish university, it was six months!) you can get into training in the mountains, wait for the weather, learn the craft gradually, and end the season with a respectable number of expeditions. If you have, as many young men of the 1930s had, only a fortnight for your alpine climbing, the more fortunate can engage guides and possibly porters to take over their own lack of carrying capacity, of climbing ability, and of local knowledge. This is simply commonsense.

The origins of guideless climbing are twofold. In the western Alps the British groups, though few in number, attained and deserved great repute. Such men as the Pilkingtons, with Eustace Hulton; Wicks, Wilson and Bradby; Mummery, Slingsby, Hastings and Collie; Hope and Kirkpatrick; were all men who could well have afforded to engage guides, but who deliberately chose not to do so. It was otherwise in the great area of the eastern Alps, an alpine region which is actually larger than the western Alps and which includes more difficult rock-climbing – even if its snow and ice climbing is not generally of the quality to be found on Mont Blanc or in the Valais or Oberland. There the characteristic climber of the 1880–1914 period was the university student of perhaps Vienna or Munich, impecunious as are all such young men, for whom guideless climbing was at least as much a necessity as a virtue. Apart from this, the lower heights involved fewer problems of weather conditions, snow techniques and so forth, so that the acro-

Overleaf: Verte from Petits Charmoz.

W. Cecil Slingsby.

batic skills which are so valuable on steep rock were the main qualities needed in a climber. It was just the same at the turn of the present century, when rock-climbing in Britain became the chief sport within the native clubs and provided the groundwork of modern climbing for us.

Sheer courage, skill, endurance and good fortune fall into no pattern. I can mention, almost at random, the brilliant feats in the mountains which illumine this connection and give no support for the theory of the supremacy of the guide which was held for so long, or for the supremacy of the amateur which is nowadays often urged. Jean Charlet with other guides made the first ascent of the Peti Dru as long ago as 1879, and he used steel pegs as abseil points on the way down, thus anticipating methods later elaborated in the eastern Alps. This climb was exceptional because no amateurs were taken. In general it is fair to say that most guides of high skill might explore routes tentatively to ensure that they were possible, in order to encourage their patrons to engage them for a 'first ascent'. Admittedly the amateurs might think out new lines for themselves, and it is almost impossible to disentangle, at this point of time, the guides' contribution in planning from that of their patrons! Alexander Burgener is associated with the first ascent of the Grépon, and Mummery himself led on the second and third, and on the first traverse of the mountain. Carson Roberts *led his guides* up the same peak: on another occasion Burgener insisted that his patron, an English amateur, lead him up the crack.

In the eastern Alps, standards of good rock-climbing, with or without pitons, were established by famous amateurs all too little known or appreciated in Britain. Von Barth, Winkler, the Zsigmondy brothers, Purtscheller, all were ahead of most climbers in that age. Yet the total contribution of the skilled guides, teamed with experienced amateurs, was still the major part of alpine climbing, and laid the solid foundation of classic routes upon which all later progress is really based. The occasional expedition to the Himalayas, the Caucasus or the Andes usually included European guides in the team.

The zenith of this style was certainly reached in the twenty years preceding the First World War. The Lochmatters and Knubel from the Zermatt valley, with such men as Geoffrey Young, H. O. Jones, V. J. E. Ryan, devised routes which were among the finest yet to be opened up. A brilliant Dolomite guide, Angelo Dibona, with his patrons the Austrian brothers Mayer, made elegant routes on his native cliffs, and then had

Joseph Knubel, a photograph taken by G. W. Young.

the opportunity of doing the same in the Chamonix district and in Dauphiné. Even beyond these first rate rock routes, an occasional sparkle of genius dazzled the mountain world. Such a one was the solo ascent by Paul Preuss of the east wall of the Guglia di Brenta, without pitons, as just one example of the tremendous standard that could be set in the eastern Alps where, incidentally, the cult of solo climbing was so often followed, though it has never developed into a popular style.

The real advent of our modern age came after the First World War. It was then that British rock-climbing moved into higher gear, foreshadowed by the ascent of the Central Buttress of Scafell in 1914. In France, GHM was founded, upon similar principles to those of the eastern alpine academic clubs and the British clubs. The development of new and severe routes in the Chamonix Aiguilles came from this energetic and enterprising new club. In Germany and Austria comparable groups developed the systems of artificial climbing devised by Dülfer before the war, in areas such as the Karwendel and the Wilderkaiser, where the rock formation both favoured and justified the use of pitons, first as abseil points, then as direct aids to ascent. The Italians, having acquired the Dolomites, followed suit. In Switzerland such clubs as the Androsace in Geneva were formed of amateurs and guides concerned with high standards of difficulty.

The decline of the Guides' Society of Chamonix had been seen after the opening of the Montanvert railway in 1908, and elsewhere the new

pattern of society, even in England, had induced changes in the system of guided climbing. True, there was no sudden change, but the greater use of crampons on ice and hard snow had removed one of the chief qualities of guides, that of cutting steps for long periods. The trend in the direction of steep rock routes narrowed the gap between the professional and the trained amateur, so that the guides in general had no longer the need to require, for their own safety, that they should take only one client. Systems developed of a small party engaging one guide, for his undoubted and necessary attributes – a knowledge of his own peaks, a knowledge of weather and of snow conditions – as leader of a party, which might split into two or three ropes, each tactically competent in the detail of a climb which the guide could direct in strategy.

It was in this period also that a few élite guides still retained their pre-eminence. Two contrasted examples must suffice – that of Armand Charlet, mayor of Argentière, sometime president of the Chamonix guides. His was perhaps the greatest name in the western Alps of the period we review, and among his many feats, which included explorations upon the great buttresses of the Grandes Jorasses, perhaps the most distinctive was the lead of the Aiguilles du Diable, in nailed boots and without the use of a single piton. He was the author of a remarkable reversal of trends, for he opened the way to brilliant amateurs becoming accepted as guides, and some of the best Chamonix guides in recent years have in fact come by that route and are not Chamoniards.

The other was the Italian, Emilio Comici, who adopted the highly mechanised systems originated by Dülfer, and whose most distinctive achievement was the first ascent in 1933 of the north wall of the Cima Grande di Lavaredo with

Hermann Steuri on North-East Ridge of Jungfrau.

Opposite: Dru.

Swiss Mountaineering School, Rosenlaui.

two other guides. He later made the second ascent, with the pitons in place, solo in under four hours. This was really the prototype of present day pioneer climbing, and it is entertaining to look back at the storm of criticism which the ascent evoked in the *Alpine Journal*. During the same period, before the Second World War, many German parties were also developing new approaches both in their own territory and in the western Alps, at the cost of a high death roll.

Modern mountaineering as carried out since 1945 accepts free and artificial climbing upon equal terms, and the remaining gap between the top amateurs and the top guides has narrowed. If, at times, it may seem that the amateurs are better than the guides, it is largely because they are prepared to push nearer to the limits of the possible in pioneering. The guides, to some extent, justifiably follow the old maxim of Melchior Anderegg . . . 'ja, es geht, aber ich gehe nicht!' ('yes, *it* goes, but I won't'). But the guides who have repeated big routes have often given salutary examples of sureness and speed. One thinks of Rébuffat on the Dru, Hermann Steuri on the north face of the Matterhorn, the Schluneggers of Wengen on the first Swiss ascent of the Eigerwand. And when a guide or a rope of guides pioneer something themselves, a masterpiece is seen. Perhaps the finest example to date, although as long ago as 1955, was Bonatti's solo climb up the south-west pillar of the Dru, with five bivouacs on the wall.

What then is the position today? First, the Alpine Club, with a single dissentient voice, has rescinded its rule that no professional guide is eligible for membership. A small matter in the context of world mountaineering, but still 'a famous victory'. Professional climbers are simply those who are fortunate enough to be able to

Opposite: Schlunegger brothers of Wengen.

devote all their time to the sport, and include not only orthodox guides to be found in every mountain valley of the alpine regions, but also professional soldiers in such units as the Alpini of Italy; the Chasseurs Alpins of France; the successors to the Kaiserjäger of Austria; the light infantry and artillery of Switzerland; and, youngest of all, the Royal Marine Commandos and Special Air Service of the British Army; they also include the instructors, mainly qualified guides, at the many mountain training schools which have been established all over the world, some ante-dating the last war. Chamonix for instance has its National School of Skiing and Mountaineering as well as the Military School serving the Chasseurs and other army units. Comici himself was in charge of the Italian Alpini school at Aosta before the war. In Switzerland, Meiringen has one of the best schools in the country, yet there are many others. Meiringen has special advantages because in addition to the great gneiss peaks of the Oberland, with its enormous glaciers, the Engelhorner, Wetterhorner, and the Eiger, all of hard limestone, offer training in techniques identical with those needed in the Dolomites and eastern Alps. Chamonix, though a superb area, is less varied in its rock.

All the opportunities for instruction in mountain work make it much easier for beginners to attain adequate competence upon which they may build such further progress as their capacities allow and their inclinations suggest.

The sport is indeed fortunate that today training schools under professional climbers have been established almost everywhere, notably in the USA.

Mountain accidents seem to be frequent, and indeed they are, because of the great number of people making expeditions. It is an essential part of the modern pattern that skilled rescue teams should operate and the cadre of professionals in this work is vital to efficiency. Sometimes, indeed, it seems that rescue teams in some valleys – Chamonix for example – are formed of too many men for the work in hand, and the control of rescue operations in Switzerland stands perhaps as the model. Here the regulations are laid down by the Swiss Alpine Club and by the Swiss government, and operate well.

I should like to conclude this very brief survey of the changing role of the professional climber with a few opinions built upon my own forty years of climbing, none of it particularly distinguished, yet all of it an essential part of a full and varied life. In this television age, mountaineering has become what it never was before – a sport for spectators. Naturally, only the highlights are shown, and the picture is distorted. It is not the five star climbs that really matter but the tremendous range of established classic routes, of every degree of difficulty. With competence, which can be reached under professional training, many thousands of climbers can and do enjoy their own selections from this vast repertoire, with guides or without. I have done a good deal of both. The occasional climb with a guide, not necessarily of the top class, is still a valuable revision of steadiness and pace for any climber. The trained mountaineer who has never made a long good quality alpine traverse with a guide, has missed a great deal. The man who is, like myself, not so young as he was and who looks back nostalgically on his guideless days, can prolong his mountain pleasures in the company of a guide, upon routes that he might think have become distinctly steeper with the years; for it remains true today, as in 1870, that 'mountaineering is after all a sport and not a duty'.

Opposite: Lionel Terray climbing in the Vercors a few weeks before his death. Bonington behind.

Chapter 5

The Distant Hills

A new chapter of mountaineering is about to be opened in Antarctica. No book of modern mountaineering is complete without a contribution by Tilman – the seaman-climber. The Americans have made nought of distance and difficulty in Alaska, using aircraft to position their parties for a number of notable assaults. Shipton's expeditions in Patagonia are among his most successful and, by way of contrast with lands of high altitude – but equally 'distant' because of their difficulty of access – are the Mountains of the Moon

MOUNTAINS OF ANTARCTICA *F.R.Brooke*

In January 1941, Sir James Clark Ross in command of HMS *Terror* and HMS *Erebus* pushed through the pack ice to become the first to see the magnificent Admiralty mountains, a panorama which will stand comparison with many views of the Himalayas and the High Andes. The Admiralty mountains are the northern extremity of a range which stretches south, flanking the western border of the Ross Sea and Ross ice shelf, for over 1,000 miles. This is but one of many ranges in Antarctica whose mountaineering possibilities are only just beginning to be appreciated.

Mount Erebus (12,450 ft), was the first major peak to be climbed. The ascent was made by members of Shackleton's Nimrod expedition in 1908 after they had finished a month's exhausting work landing their stores, building their hut, and generally preparing for the winter. After thirty-six hours' hectic preparation, a six man party set out without previous mountaineering experience or proper equipment. The sledge and the heavy awkward tent poles were left behind at their second camp and the three man 'support' party, which had no crampons, had to carry a three man reindeer skin sleeping-bag, a heavy cumbersome load for one man. The summit was gained at 10 am on March 10, and they became the first men to look down into the crater which they estimated to be 900 ft deep and half a mile wide. Only one man failed to reach the summit; he had frostbitten feet from wearing ski-boots the previous day.

The lack of suitable footwear for climbing in very low temperatures was one of the reasons

HMS *Protector* off Smith Island, Antarctic Peninsula.

which delayed the start of real mountaineering in Antarctica. There were other reasons. Just as early travellers in the Alps made science an excuse for their ventures, so have polar explorers. The underlying urge of Shackleton, Scott and Fuchs was almost certainly to adventure, to explore, to make a notable 'first'; but each man brought in science to justify the large sums of money that must be spent to enable anyone to visit the Antarctic. Similarly individual expedition members out on journeys were responsible for carrying out specific tasks which did not normally include climbing mountains. Moreover, to be seen for the first time, the normal desire is to travel as far as possible. When using dogs this means cutting down the weight of everything which is not man- and dog-food. Dogs still need food, even if they have spent the day resting while a mountain is climbed. Mountaineering and long unsupported dog sledge journeys do not really go together.

There are thus three problems to be solved in Antarctic mountaineering – equipment to combat the climatic conditions, access, and attitude of mind.

The survey and geological parties of the Norwegian–Swedish–British Expedition to Queen Maud Land 1950–2 were the first to do good mountaineering. They solved the boot problem by wearing a thin rubber sock, or a thin plastic bag, over the bare foot and then two or three pairs of thick wool socks inside a US Army ski-mountaineering boot. This effectively converted it into a vapour barrier boot. Access to the mountains was solved by working from a large depot established by mechanical vehicles in a mountain range of limited extent. They considered that to climb mountains was an essential part of their job in order to investigate the rock formations and establish survey stations on the summits. Many fine climbs of alpine standard on rock, snow and ice were carried out despite a load of rocks or a theodolite on the climbers' backs.

Profiting by Himalayan developments members of the New Zealand party of the Trans-Antarctic Expedition 1957–8 were equipped with high altitude boots. A large number of mountains were climbed by the several survey and geological parties who, although they used dogs, were supported by aircraft; the majority of these mountains were simple walks, but some good climbs were done including two major ascents. In February 1957 B. Gunn, A. Heine and G. Warren climbed Mount Harmsworth (9,090 ft) in the Worcester Range, direct from a camp on the Skelton Glacier. The height to be gained was over 8,000 ft and the horizontal distance was considerable. This 'tour de force' took them twenty-six hours. Eleven months later, in January 1958, Brooke and Gunn climbed Mount Huggins (12,870 ft), the southernmost of the high peaks of the Royal Society Range. They left their dogs at about 5,000 ft and established a light camp at about 8,000 ft, from which they climbed to the summit in eight hours.

Since 1958 New Zealand parties have made good use of the easy access afforded by American aircraft flying to the air strip in McMurdo Sound by sending out several small summer expeditions. These expeditions have normally included some experienced mountaineers and many fine climbs have been done for scientific reasons, pleasure, or a mixture of the two. These climbs have been characterised by length rather than difficulty and climbing days of anything up to thirty-two hours have been recorded. These long climbs are indicative of the difficulty of estimating height and distance in the clear atmosphere, the horizontal distances in particular being so very much greater than in any alpine area.

It is rash to generalise on conditions in so vast an area, but in the main the Antarctic summer is fine with very little snowfall, especially away from the coast. It is of course cold – the equivalent of mid winter in the Alps – and all too frequently windy. Gloves are normally essential, though on rare windless days they can sometimes be dispensed with. On the other hand hard wind-blown snow, excellent for crampons throughout the twenty-four hours, is normal. There are some local windless areas where soft snow lies, such as the Axel Heiberg Glacier, Amundsen's route to the plateau. In the Axel Heiberg avalanches caused by falling seracs are common, but elsewhere they are seldom, if ever, seen. All in all, remembering the twenty-four hours of daylight and the generally settled, if windy, weather, climbing conditions are not at all bad.

The conditions in Grahamland and the neighbouring islands are very different. Grahamland is much farther north and therefore warmer. It juts out towards South America, into the prevailing westerly winds laden with moisture from the South Pacific, and consequently receives a heavy snowfall. The weather is most uncertain and is often bad or very bad.

The mountains on the west coast and adjacent islands are superb. Some, although they are only 2,000 or 3,000 ft high, look like replicas of those in Patagonia – vertical rock drowned with ice. It is not easy to find a safe place to land because ice cliffs plunge into the sea over much of the

Opposite above: Mountains of Victoria Land seen from Mt Suess.
Opposite below: Umanak region, Greenland.
Overleaf: Wind – the Antarctic traveller's enemy.

coastline, nor is it easy to travel along these coastal glaciers. Consequently most of these bases have been built on rocky islets off the main peninsula or islands. Owing to the comparatively warm weather, the frequent gales and the tides, the sea ice is rarely safe for travel and boating in summer is equally dangerous because of the weather and drifting ice.

These conditions have severely restricted the mountaineering activities of the occupants of the permanent British, Argentinean and Chilean bases in the area, although some good climbs have been done, particularly since 1955. The only safe means of access is from a well-found ship.

This fact has been put to good use by the Royal Navy. Their ice patrol ship, HMS *Protector*, has the additional advantage of carrying helicopters and so can land parties in places and in conditions which would be impossible by any other means.

In December 1960 a party of Royal Marines led by Captain V. N. Stevenson made a rush attempt on Mount Paget (9,625 ft), the highest peak in South Georgia. The conditions in South Georgia are very similar to those in Grahamland except that the temperatures are higher and the weather is worse. The short history of climbing in South Georgia is peppered with accounts of hurricanes lasting a week or more with winds up to 100 knots, of tent poles breaking and tents giving way under the incessant battering of wet or frozen drift. Stevenson's party only had five days to spare. Luckily their attempt coincided with a spell of reasonable weather, and Stevenson, Lt. Cdr. M. K. Burley and Corporal R. Todd were able to reach the far west peak in a final climb of fourteen hours, with a bivouac on the descent.

Burley made use of this experience by leading

Mountains seen from Horseshoe Island, west coast of Grahamland.

Anvers Island, west coast of Grahamland.

Opposite: Evighedsfjord, Greenland.

Following Shackleton's tracks above Fortuna Bay, South Georgia.

Mt Fagerli.

a Combined Services Expedition to South Georgia in 1964–5. After depots had been established by helicopter at strategic points, the party was put ashore in King Haakon Bay to follow Shackleton's route across the island after his epic open boat journey from Elephant Island. It is noteworthy that the journey which Shackleton and his two companions, with no equipment except a carpenter's adze, a rope and a primus, accomplished in thirty-six hours, took this well-found party of ten men fifteen days. The price of sufficient reserves of food and fuel to withstand atrocious weather is inevitably slow travel.

Burley's party later made the first ascent of Mount Paget, (9,625 ft), and Mount Sugartop, (7,623 ft), and then succeeded in crossing the Allardyce Range, a very notable achievement.

Big Ben, a 9,000 ft volcano on Heard Island 53°10′S 73°35′E has even worse weather than South Georgia. Apart from crevasses hidden with fiendish cunning there are no technical difficulties. In 1963 a party of three led by W. Deacock found a practicable route, but they were caught in a prolonged and severe storm in their tent at 7,500 ft and after various misadventures were lucky to get out alive.

Deacock returned in 1965 and was landed with four companions from a 63 ft schooner which had been sailed from Australia by H. W. Tilman with an amateur crew. This in itself was no mean feat. Profiting by experience Deacock set up his advanced camp at only 4,000 ft and stocked it with three weeks food. After only four days of siege they were able to take advantage of a fine

day and reached the summit after a climb of twelve and a half hours.

In 1966–7 the first purely mountaineering expedition visited Antarctica. Their objective was the Sentinel Mountains which were seen from the air by Lincoln Ellsworth during his Trans-Continental flight in 1935. They were first visited for scientific purposes in 1957–8, and have since been established as the highest mountains in Antarctica. They are an extensive range with some magnificent peaks which rise about 6,000 ft above the surrounding glaciers.

The ten man American Mountaineering Expedition led by N.B. Clinch was flown in, together with a motor toboggan for local transport. In six weeks they climbed Vinson Massif (16,860 ft), the highest in Antarctica, and five other fine peaks. The hardest climb was Mount Tyree (16,290 ft). The route chosen lay over Mount Gardner (15,380 ft), and down to the col between the two peaks. Three camps were established above glacier level and the final climb along a $2\frac{1}{2}$ mile ridge was very difficult.

The last ten years has shown a steady quickening of interest, and many more mountains have been climbed than I have mentioned. Now that the conditions in many varied parts of the Antarctic are known and equipment has been developed to combat them, we can expect much harder climbs to be attempted in the future.

Antarctic: crevasse.

Opposite above: Descending from Mt Huggins.
Opposite below: High camp on Mt Huggins.

Antarctic blizzard.

Arrigetch Peaks, N. Alaska.

ALASKA *Terris Moore*

The 'golden age' of mountaineering in Alaska, that of first ascents combined with geographical exploration, ended a generation ago. A second and very different golden age however, that of modern mountaineering, began immediately after the Second World War, and is in full swing today.

The discovery and climbing of Alaska's great peaks – those more lofty than the highest to be found anywhere in the other forty-nine states of the USA – essentially constitutes that first period of Alaskan mountaineering. Alaska has a dozen such giants, four of them on the boundary with Canada: Mount St Elias which rises 18,000 ft at the point where the Alaskan 'Panhandle' commences; then to its east and south, Mounts Vancouver (15,850 ft), Hubbard (15,015 ft) and Fairweather (15,300 ft). With the Pacific Ocean lapping within fifteen to twenty miles of their bases, these are clearly the highest coastal mountains in the world; and in that sense the most spectacular.

The exploration of Alaska for a century and a half had been confined to marine charting and river travel, until in 1890–1 I. C. Russell, the US government scientist, attempted the ascent of St Elias, to ascertain from a high aerial view what lay in the interior to its immediate north: 'a vast region which no one had yet beheld'. He 'expected to look down upon a comparatively low, wooded country, with lakes and rivers and perhaps some signs of aboriginal human habitation'. But to his astonishment, he beheld only vast glaciers and great mountains – among them Canada's huge Mount Logan (19,850 ft), which

Arrigetch Peaks of Brooks Range.

he thereby discovered and named – running so far as his eye could see, through to 'two prominent mountain ranges – 200 miles away – which must be in the vicinity of Mount Wrangell'. In this sweep he was the first to see and name Mount Bear (14,850 ft). The Italian Duke of the Abruzzi, in 1897, employing alpine guides, first reached the summit of St Elias, and from this higher elevation described and named far distant Mount Bona (16,420 ft).

Mount McKinley's vast height (20,320 ft) was not recognised, nor the mountain officially named, until 1896; its companions, Mounts Foraker (17,395 ft) and Hunter (14,580 ft), not long thereafter. The great peaks of the Wrangell Range, originally described with some confusion in 1885, were finally in the 1890s mapped as Mounts Blackburn (16,523 ft) and Sanford (16,200 ft). But not until 1930, during the first ascent of Mount Bona, was the last major geographical discovery in Alaska made: today's University Range, the highest point of which, University Peak, is in the 14,500 ft class. The last three of Alaska's great mountains to be climbed – Mount Bear the most remote and least interesting (being a high flat plateau), and Mount Hunter and University Peak the only two of any real technical difficulty – were not ascended until the 1950s – thus concluding the exploratory period.

Modern mountaineering in Alaska begins with three events, all featured in the 1947 issue of the *American Alpine Journal*.

(1) The advent of climbers not only able to cope

Opposite: Shot Tower, Arrigetch Peaks.

with routes of great technical difficulty, but young and energetic enough to do them: the expeditions led by Fred Beckey beginning with the first ascents of Devil's Thumb (9,077 ft) and Kate's Needle (10,002 ft), marker peaks on the boundary with Canada up the Stikine River.
(2) the first 'new route' climbed on any Alaskan peak: the ascent of Mount St Elias from the south-west (Abruzzi's had been from the east), made by the Harvard Mountaineering Club.
(3) The article published by Bradford Washburn entitled *Mount McKinley from the North and West*, proposing new routes of interesting difficulty on that giant peak. This article represented an innovation in alpine journalism; for the proposed new routes on McKinley had never been approached by qualified climbers, Washburn's route suggestions being worked out entirely from his own aerial photographs viewed under the stereoscope. That these routes were soon successfully climbed verified their original significance: Washburn himself indeed pioneered the first of these, leading the West Buttress climb of McKinley in 1951.

Aircraft had been used before the Second World War to aid mountaineering expeditions – in 1932, apparently the first time anywhere, on the Carpé-Beckwith cosmic ray research effort at Mount McKinley; and by Washburn and Bates (with pilot Bob Reeve out of Valdez) on their remarkable traverse of Mount Lucania in 1937. But it was not until the post-war technical development of 'ski-wheel' gear, convertible in flight from wheels to skis and vice versa, that it became possible to give modern air support to mountaineering expeditions. With one of these new devices on his Piper Super Cub, the writer as pilot was able to land four of Washburn's 1951 party on Mount McKinley's Kahiltna Glacier at

Overleaf: Mt St Elias looking North-West.
Opposite: Summit of Mt Crillon seen from north-west from over Malspina Glacier.

7,500 ft, and, after the climb, to take off all eight members of that party, one by one, direct from the 10,000 ft level back to civilisation. This has now become the standard professional practice in Alaska, pilots Sheldon and Wilson having successfully transported innumerable mountaineering parties in this fashion – not to by-pass technical climbing problems, but to eliminate many tedious days of approach marching.

The visit of Heinrich Harrer in 1954 marked the first arrival in Alaska's mountains of a climber capable of dealing with routes on an Eigerwand scale of *extreme* difficulty. His first ascent, with Beckey and Meybohm, of spectacular Mount Deborah, the 12,540 ft showpiece of the Hayes Range, is reported by them as 'the most sensational ice climb' any of these three powerful climbers had ever undertaken.

Washburn continued to write articles in the *American Alpine Journal*, proposing new routes on Mount McKinley. And among those now attracted by these articles was Ricardo Cassin, who in July 1961, led five members of the Italian Alpine Club on a nineteen-day first ascent of McKinley's south face – a route of *extreme* difficulty, in places Italian 'grade 5 superior' and '40 metre grade 6'. Similarly Lionel Terray was attracted to Mount Huntington, and in May 1964, led seven members of the Club Alpin Français in the first ascent of this nearby 12,240 ft very difficult peak.

Its second ascent was made the next year, via a new route, the west face, by a Harvard Mountaineering Club party, in whose account of this

and their 1966 climbs in the dramatically impressive Cathedral Spires region of 'vertical walls, pinnacles, obelisks' appears this summary:

> There are not many unclimbed prizes left in Alaska – but there are hundreds of new routes to be done, direct, challenging lines that thrill the mountaineer's heart. Of all the peaks in that great land, only McKinley has received proper attention (a dozen routes and a winter ascent have now been done) . . . But . . . ridges lie waiting on Foraker, buttresses on Hunter beg to be climbed.

And a final line which might equally apply to the inspiring Granite Towers of Arrigetch in the Brooks Range:

> What if we had climbed a certain mountain? It is still there, surrounded on every side by summits no man has ever visited, offering, as only the wilderness can, this world's last illusion of paradise.

Granite Peaks, Brooks Range – Badile, Disneyland, Citadel.

Overleaf: Mt McKinley from Ruth Amphitheatre Base Camp.

Iceberg study.

GREENLAND – SAILING TO CLIMB *H.W. Tilman*

Slocum – himself no mean judge of enterprise – said of his father 'he was the sort of man who, if wrecked on a desolate island, would find his way home if he had a jack-knife and could find a tree'. It could equally be said of Tilman 'tell him of a mountain ten thousand miles away across the sea, and he will sail the sea and climb the mountain'.

Obviously a man who likes to sail to the foot of his climb can forget the Alps or the Himalayas. He must look for regions where the glaciers come down to the sea, places that are usually remote, inaccessible, uninhabited. So much the better. There are, for example, the Patagonian Andes, Tierra del Fuego, South Georgia, the South Shetlands, or sub-antarctic islands like Kerguelen and Heard Island; but to reach such remote spots there is, to misquote Prince Hal, an intolerable deal of sea to one half-pennyworth of mountain. In the northern hemisphere, accessible in a small boat and comparatively near, are Spitsbergen, Baffin Island, and, of course, Greenland. Having visited most of these places I believe that the sea-going mountaineer will find his ideal in Greenland, where Arctic waters beat upon a wild coast, a coast cleft with fjords and studded with mountains; where in summer one enjoys continuous daylight, the delicate tints of northern skies and hills, together with the romance and excitement of icebergs and pack-ice seen at close quarters from the deck of a small boat.

Urged on by a friend, Dr. H. I. Drever, *Mischief*'s first Greenland voyage in 1961 was to

Opposite: Sehesteds fjord.
Opposite above: Mischief amongst the ice.

Overleaf: Stauning Alps.

Staunings Alps.

the Umanak region where, according to him, the scenery was grander, the icebergs bigger, and where the few inhabitants still followed to some extent the Eskimo way of life. Umanak in N. lat. 71, well inside the Arctic circle, seemed to a Greenland novice to be rather far north. We had our sights on a peak of 7,500 ft (reputedly the highest in West Greenland) on the Qioqe peninsula, but were forestalled by an Italian party led by that remarkable man Piero Ghiglioni, then aged 76. They climbed this Punta Italia from sea level in a day, and later two more peaks. Though younger in years, my companion, E. H. Marriott, and I were more senile and accomplished less. Buzzing like elderly bees from flower to flower, from Qioqe peninsula to the equally mountainous island of Upernivik, looking for peaks within our feeble grasp, we climbed only two.

In 1962 we had in view Mount Raleigh (5,200 ft), a peak on the Cumberland peninsula of Baffin Island, named four hundred years ago and still unclimbed. Since the Baffin Island coast is not free of ice until late summer we had time, before attending to Mount Raleigh, to visit Evighedsfjord on the West Greenland coast in N. lat 66. Roger Tufft and I managed to climb four peaks, the highest (6,995 ft) actually having a name, Angssaussat. Foiled by ice on our first attempt to reach Baffin Island, at last on 20 August we anchored in Exeter Sound, the place where in 1585 John Davis, the great Elizabethan seaman-explorer, had recorded: 'We lay under a brave mount, the cliffs whereof were orient as

Halvdan anchorage, Skjoldungen fjord.

gold. This mount we named Mount Raleigh.' Looking at it from the sea we had no doubts about John Davis's Mount Raleigh, but the map-makers had conferred the name on a lesser peak hard by. We therefore had to climb both. Later the Canadian Survey Department readily agreed to transfer the name to where we judged it rightly belonged and to call the lesser peak Mount Mischief.

In 1963 we once more followed in the wake of John Davis, using the west coast of Greenland as a stepping stone, so to speak, to higher things. Having rounded Cape Farewell, so named by Davis, and called at Godthaab (Davis's 'Gilbert Sound'), we sailed close under the black 1,000 ft high headland which he had named Sanderson's Hope. This headland, in N.lat 72·47, was Davis's farthest point north. Sanderson, a London merchant, had been his principal backer in his search for the North-West Passage. Up here the Greenland ice-cap comes down to the sea and there are no coastal mountains. We went on west across Baffin Bay to Bylot Island, a mountainous island rising to 6,500 ft. The mountains are too rounded to be of interest; instead Bruce Reid and I crossed the island on foot, an arduous journey of fourteen days mostly through deplorably soft snow.

The east coast of Greenland is as mountainous as the west coast and the approach to it is a sterner challenge. Owing to the presence of pack-ice the approach in a small boat to anywhere north of Cape Dyer, where the big mountains lie, is pretty well ruled out except perhaps in

September or October – late either for climbing or for returning in moderate comfort across the North Atlantic. In 1964 our objective was Skjöldungen fjord, an untouched and highly mountainous fjord about 100 miles south of Angmagssalik, which is near Cape Dyer. On our way there via the Faeroes and Iceland, Roger Coward and I climbed the new volcanic island of Surtsey, an island that had risen from under the sea, belching smoke and flame, in November 1963. It was then about 400 ft high, active and still rising. Mountaineers are avid for first ascents. This first ascent by a British party has unfortunately since been invalidated by a further rise to 800 ft on the part of Surtsey. We never reached Skjöldungen fjord. Approaching Angmagssalik in the wake of a 4,000 ton cargo vessel, preceded by the miniature ice-breaker *Ejnar Mikkelsen*, *Mischief* was nipped by two floes and suffered some sprung planks. For three weeks the ice held us prisoner in Angmagssalik while we repaired the damage and climbed two neighbouring peaks. 'Poljemsfjeld' had on it a small cairn in which were records of previous ascents by two Germans in 1931 and by two Danes in 1954.

In 1965 we reached Skjöldungen fjord with little trouble. Ice conditions vary from year to year. It is largely luck, though something of what may be expected can be learnt from the ice maps compiled monthly by the meteorological office, Bracknell. The fjord fairly bristled with mountains and I regret we did not set about them with more vigour. My companion, Brian Holloway, had done no climbing, and his ice-axe, like the Dutchman's anchor, had been left behind.

Opposite above: Glacier on Upernivik Island.
Opposite below: Mountains south of Evighedsfjord.

Together with my timidity, this led to meagre results. We climbed but two of the easier peaks and one in Sehesteds fjord farther south. Though this fjord also abounds in mountains it is too choked with glacier ice to be pleasant for a small boat party. Narrow fjords that have glaciers descending into them direct from the ice-cap are likely to be filled with floes.

Thus these five Greenland visits were remarkable chiefly for showing how little can be achieved if one tries hard enough. Of course, a party of two climbing in an uninhabited region, unsupported, with the safety of their boat and its safe return always in mind, must be prudent. Nevertheless the opportunities open to a small party climbing from their own boat need not be judged by our example. Most of the anchorages in the fjords are safe enough, so that leaving, say, only two behind as ship-keepers, a young and active party of four could quit the boat for a month at a time and roam far inland. The only mountains out of reach to such a party would be the Stauning Alps where, owing to ice conditions on the east coast, a small boat would not get within striking distance. If remoteness and inaccessibility be his criterion, Greenland can be regarded as such only by a man who turns his back on modern sea and air transport. Many mountaineers, mostly of the old-fashioned kind, regard the approach to their chosen mountains as something to be savoured lingeringly, as satisfying in its way as the mountains themselves, especially if the approach is arduous and difficult. This, of course, implies time, a commodity that few nowadays can spare. To anyone with both time and a small boat a voyage to Greenland offers, certainly a lingering, sometimes a challenging approach to the finest small scale mountains in the world.

Bakonjo porters.

THE MOUNTAINS OF THE MOON *Rennie Bere*

More than two thousand years ago there were wise men in ancient Greece who realised that the Nile rose from snow-covered mountains far down in the heart of Africa. In the second century AD, Ptolemy placed them with considerable accuracy and used the name Mountains of the Moon. But until Sir Henry Stanley actually saw the Ruwenzori, less than a hundred years ago, the western world simply refused to believe in their existence. This late discovery resulted partly from their situation, far removed from any of the old caravan routes. But it was also due to the cover of cloud and haze which is almost permanent and hides the range completely for months on end. Access to the base of the mountains is now easy. The strange weather conditions remain to protect the summits so that climbing problems today are much the same as they were fifty years ago. No amount of modern technique will enable you to see your peak when it is completely hidden in the mist, nor will it help you to find your way across a Ruwenzori bog.

The cloud cover, in combination with the equatorial position, is also responsible for the astonishing size, growth and luxuriance of the plant life. Floral zones succeed one another as height is gained: tree-ferns in the low mountain forests; hollow-stemmed mountain bamboos forty feet high; gigantic heather trees, as tall as pines, cushioned in moss and festooned with long, grey tufts of Old Man's Beard. The alpine zone proper starts above all this at about 12,000 ft. Dominated by giant Groundsels, the size of small trees, and Lobelias with flower-spikes of nearly twenty feet,

'There is an air of quiet imperturbability about the high Ruwenzori.'

this part of the Ruwenzori is turned into a region of outstanding beauty by occasional flowering St John's Wort trees and by the Helichrysum Everlastings. These lovely flowers, very similar to the familiar garden variety, grow in unbroken stands which cover several acres, their woody stems creating a tangle almost impossible to penetrate. At all levels, indeed, movement is seriously inhibited by the mud, the dense and rotting vegetation as well as the fallen tree-trunks which cover much of the ground. They combine to take the rhythm out of your steps, and to make the walk up to the peaks something of a nightmare relieved only by the beauty and exceptional interest of the fantastic surroundings.

The whole range is immensely rugged. Streams cascade down many of the steeper slopes. Deep-cut, ice-eroded valleys radiate outwards from the higher peaks and are blocked, at intervals, to produce either glacier-lakes or the enormous bogs which are so typical of the Ruwenzori – not only do these bogs turn whole valleys into impenetrable morasses, somehow or other they manage to cling on to near-vertical mountainsides. The glaciers are ice-caps rather than ice-rivers. They are more extensive than those of either Kilimanjaro or Mount Kenya, both higher than the Ruwenzori and the only other mountains in tropical Africa with permanent snow and ice. Great cornices, underpinned by enormous icicles, decorate the more exposed ice-ridges at the highest levels. Rock peaks stand clear above the snows.

The animal life, though less in evidence than

Overleaf: Ruwenzori stream.

The highest peaks of the Mountains of the Moon – Alexandra and Margherita Peaks, Mt Stanley.

the vegetation, is worthy of this extraordinary setting. Buffaloes and elephants roam the lower forests where chimpanzees build their nests high up in the taller trees. Monkeys of several kinds occur as well as a few of the smaller antelopes. Giant forest hogs break trails through undergrowth which no human can hope to penetrate. Leopards have been known to enter expedition tents. Among numerous smaller creatures is the Ruwenzori Hyrax whose cries shatter the silence of the hills. Hyraxes look rather like alpine marmots and are extremely plentiful, particularly in the heather forest. They are preyed upon by leopards and hunted by the Bakonjo tribesmen who eat their flesh and make use of their skins – the Bakonjo, who live around the base of the mountains and on the lower slopes, serve as expedition porters and do this job admirably in spite of the prevailing conditions. There is a molerat with a wedge-shaped head but no ears, no eyes, no neck and no tail. And in 1953 the Ruwenzori otter-shrew, which looks like a minute otter and was previously unknown to science, was discovered accidentally in one of the western rivers.

Many of the birds stay hidden in the thickets. But small flocks of the glorious Ruwenzori Turaco, blue and green with a crimson crest, sometimes fly across an open valley or crawl squirrel-like along a branch. Long-tailed Dartmouth Sunbirds probe for nectar when the lobelias are in flower. Buzzards, falcons and occasionally eagles soar among the peaks.

With such natural riches, it is not surprising

Opposite: The range is never absolutely clear of cloud. Savoiā Peak, Mt Stanley.

that some of the more important expeditions of recent years should have had scientific rather than climbing objectives. The complicated geology of the range was investigated in 1951 by parties of British and Belgian geologists working in close collaboration under the leadership of Professor Kennedy – though the detail of this is still in dispute, it can be said that the Ruwenzori is an upthrust connected with the Rift Valley system and is not volcanic in origin as are most of the higher mountains in tropical Africa. An overall survey of the range, achieved by means of air photography followed up by ground control, was completed in 1955. And, between 1957 and 1959, a comprehensive examination of the glaciers was made by the university of East Africa. There have also been several small botanical and zoological collecting expeditions adding steadily to knowledge.

In spite of the mist and the haze, tolerable climbing weather does occur. Even if the range is never absolutely clear, you often find the peaks in sunshine above the clouds. Fog builds up with surprising suddenness, however, and cannot be anticipated. This restricts climbing but does not prevent it. In other respects the weather is no worse than it is in many other mountain regions; it does not rain every day of the year as you often read.

All the main peaks had been climbed before 1945; and a few routes, hard by classical standards, had been done. Most of these climbs have been repeated. Others have been made: for example, two routes on the west face of Mount Stanley, the highest mountain in the range, by that indomitable Italian veteran Piero Ghiglione. Then, in 1956, Jeremy Smith and T. E. Fletcher were lucky enough to hit upon eighteen days of almost continuously good weather when well placed for the higher peaks. They climbed, for the first time, a prominent pinnacle known as Great Tooth, repeated two of the hardest of the earlier routes and made one great climb of their own; this was the splendid scimitar-shaped ridge which gives Mount Stanley its characteristic northern outline. By a tragic coincidence, and only a short time after these climbs, Smith was killed in the Alps, and Ghiglione was killed in a motor accident in Italy.

It is probably correct to describe those few days in 1956 as the climax of mountaineering achievement in the Ruwenzori. Most parties have been content to repeat old routes or seek the obvious way up lesser peaks or unclimbed faces. No one has yet found it either possible or necessary to move beyond the traditional methods. Perhaps this is as it should be. The conditions and the natural wonders, not the technical climbing problems, provide the range with its peculiar quality. These occur nowhere else. There is an aura of imperturbability, a pervading stillness, about the high places of the Ruwenzori. There is an extraordinary feeling of remoteness, more intense than on many greater ranges, as if you genuinely were upon another planet. This is the real mystery of the Mountains of the Moon.

Opposite: Patagonian glacier snout.
Overleaf above: Peak at head of Brook's Bay.
Overleaf below: Argentinian ponies on the pampas. Fitzroy the highest peak; Cerro Torre on the left.
Overleaf opposite: Christmas Eve 1963 at an altitude of four and a half thousand feet on the North Patagonian ice-cap. The unnamed peak is estimated by Shipton to just exceed 9,000 ft.

View north from summit of Cerro Don Bosco.

THE PATAGONIAN ANDES AND CORDILLERA DARWIN*

E.E.Shipton

I THE PATAGONIAN ANDES

For any mountaineer willing to face the prospect of rough weather conditions, the Patagonian Andes offer a wide field of fresh endeavour in a strange and very beautiful environment. In the northern section (Lat. 40°S. – 45°S.) the range is comparatively low, and broken by many rivers which rise in the east and flow through it to the Pacific. It contains several fine volcanic peaks, such as Lanin (12,390 ft) and El Tronador (11,253 ft) as well as a number of small groups, many of which have not yet been visited. Between Lat. 46°S. and 52°S., a distance of 420 miles, there is a continuous chain of heavily glaciated mountains, broken only at one point, where it is cut by Canal Baker, one of the longest of the fjords on the west coast.

Though the main features of this chain have been mapped by aerial photography on a scale of 1:250,000, a great deal of it has not been explored on the ground, while only a small proportion of the peaks have been climbed. The chief reason for this is the climate, which is notorious: savage winds blow from the north-west, sometimes for weeks at a stretch, precipitation is heavy and protracted, while fine spells are rare and usually brief. Most parts of the region, too, are difficult to reach. The coast immediately west of the range is split by a complex network of fjords, many of them blocked by glacier ice, and it is virtually uninhabited throughout its entire length. Even on the eastern side some areas can only be approached by water, and because of the wind, the use of small boats is apt to be dangerous. Many of the

* The term Patagonia refers to that part of the mainland of South America south of the Rio Negro in Latitude 40°S.

Opposite: The Fortress: climbed for the first time on 5 January 1968 by Ian Clough's party.

Snout of the three miles wide Upsola glacier.

glaciers are so broken in their lower reaches that travel on them is not a practicable proposition, and they are often flanked by dense nothofagus forest. The tree-line is about 3,000 ft, higher in the northern part of the range, lower in the southern. In exposed areas the trees are stunted and twisted by the wind into a tangle of trunks and branches often very difficult to penetrate.

In the region north of Canal Baker, the dominant feature is an extensive ice basin known as the Hielo Patagonico del Norte. It is largely surrounded by mountains, including some beautiful granite peaks which have never been attempted. Glaciers radiating from the basin flow in every direction through gaps in the mountains; several of those on the western side reach the sea on broad fronts. Monte San Valentin (12,716 ft), in the northern part of the region, is the highest peak in Patagonia; after several unsuccessful attempts it was climbed in 1952 by an Argentine party led by O. Meiling. Cerro Arenales (11,277 ft), at the southern end of the basin, was climbed in 1958 by a Japanese–Chilean expedition. Apart from these two, very few peaks of the area have been climbed. The region was traversed from north-west to south-east in 1963–4 by E. Garcia, C. Marangunic, M. Gomez and E. Shipton.

To the south-east, between Rio Baker and Rio Pascua, stands the isolated massif of Monte San Lorenzo, the highest point of which was reached in 1943 by a party led by A. de Agostini. It contains a number of fine granite aiguilles, most of which are unclimbed.

South of Canal Baker lies the Hielo Patagonico

Cerro Arenales, North Patagonian ice-cap.

del Sur, another vast icefield, similar to its neighbour across the fjord, though it is larger and can be more truly termed an 'ice-cap'. It is the only one in existence outside the polar regions. Its many glaciers flow down to Lagos O'Higgins, Viedma and Argentino on the east and to the Pacific fjords on the west. Near the centre, an active volcano, Lautaro, rises above the ice to a height of 11,000 ft. The best-known area and the most easily accessible lies to the west of Lagos Viedma and Argentino; many of the peaks there have been climbed. Overlooking Lago Viedma, well to the east of the main axis of the range, there is a group of spectacular granite peaks. The ascents of the highest of these, Cerro Fitzroy (11,077 ft), by L. Terray and G. Magnone in 1952, and of its neighbour Cerro Torre (9,908 ft) by T. Egger and C. Maestri in 1959, are regarded by some as among the finest feats in mountaineering history. In 1960–1 a party of four led by E. Shipton made a sledge journey over the whole length of the ice-cap from Canal Baker to Lago Argentino. The first crossing of the range was made farther south, between Calvo Fjord and Lago Argentino; this was achieved in 1956 by a party led by H. W. Tilman.

West of Lago Argentino the range is narrow, and at one place only five miles separate the western arm of the lake from Pacific waters; the glacier col between has not been crossed. To the south, however, the range expands and contains one of the largest glaciers in South America. On the eastern side of this region there is another set of challenging granite peaks, grouped around

Cerro Paine (ca. 10,000 ft). Perhaps the most notable achievement here has been the ascent of the Central Tower in 1963 by C. Bonington and D. Whillans.

TIERRA DEL FUEGO

Nearly all the high mountains of Tierra del Fuego are situated on a narrow, uninhabited peninsula stretching 150 miles westward from the south-west corner of the island. It is entirely Chilean territory. Like all the Pacific coastline of Patagonia, it is deeply indented by fjords; many of them, stretching into the heart of the range, are spectacular. The main massif is known as the Cordillera Darwin, covering an area which would accommodate the Mont Blanc and Pennine ranges of the Alps and the Bernese Oberland. It is very heavily glaciated, and most of the principal ice-streams reach the sea. The highest peak, Monte Darwin, is about 8,700 ft, and there are many others approaching that height. The lower slopes of the mountains, where they are not glaciated, are mostly covered with thick forest, though ridges exposed to the westerly winds are often bare. The forest extends to 1,500 ft above sea-level, and often presents a difficult barrier.

If anything, the climate here is even worse than in the Patagonian Andes, for the peninsula is lashed by the westerly gales which rage around Cape Horn and bring long periods of evil weather. This again is the main reason why the range is so little known. In 1898, Martin Conway made an unsuccessful attempt on Monte Sarmiento (7,370 ft), a western outlier of the range,

Paine Hut (tents could not withstand the wind).

Opposite: Trench excavated by wind.

Overleaf: Approach to the Cordillera Darwin, Tierra del Fuego.

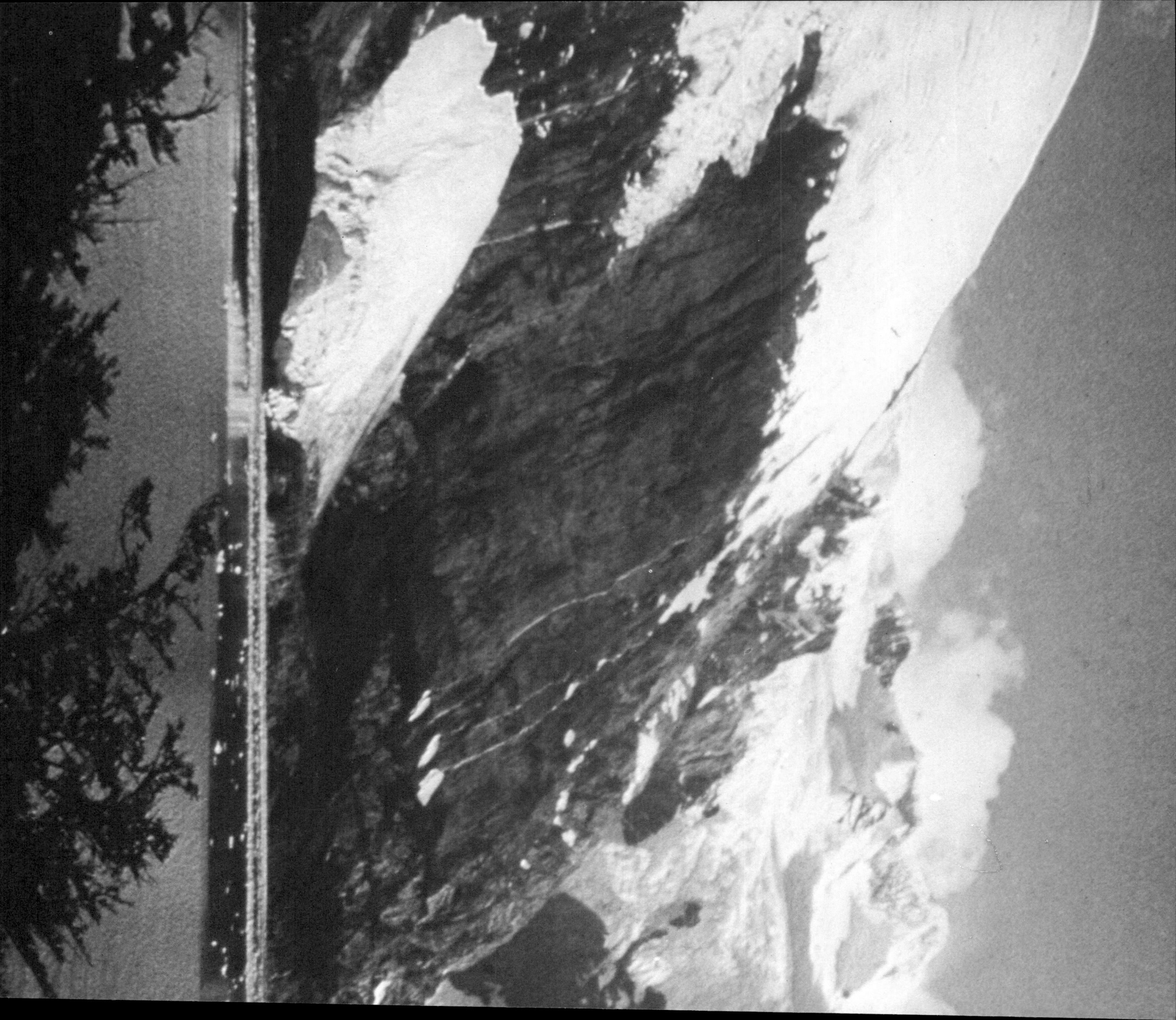

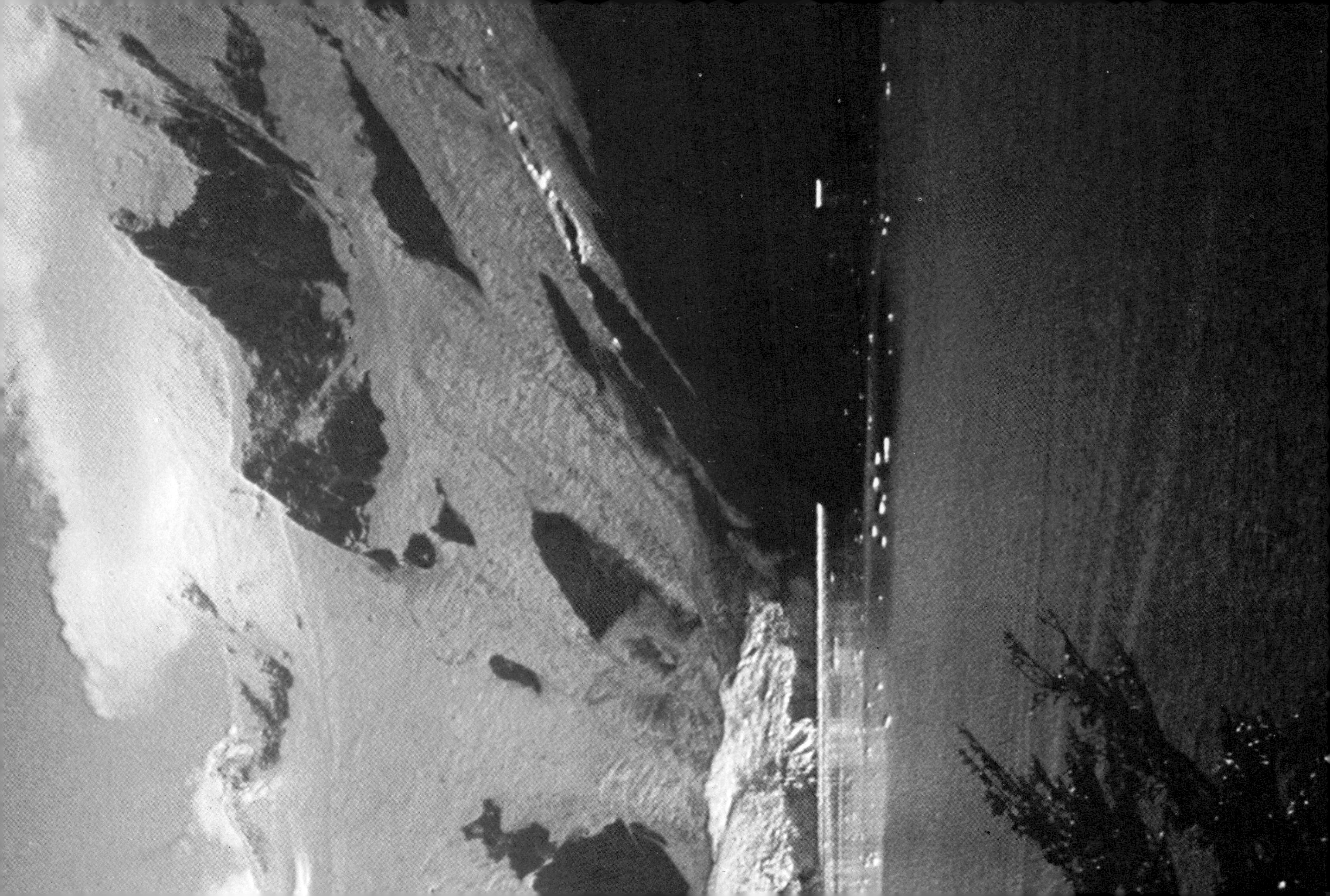

A 'gentle' breeze blows on the Col between the Don Bosco and Murallon.

then thought to be the highest peak in Tierra del Fuego. Its beautiful ice spire was a well-known landmark for the early navigators of the Magellan Straits. After several subsequent attempts, Sarmiento was eventually climbed in 1956 by the Italians, C. Mauri and C. Maffei. In 1962 an expedition composed of E. Garcia, C. Marangunic, F. Vivanco and E. Shipton made the first substantial penetration into the central part of the range, which they crossed from Brooks Bay to the Beagle Channel, and climbed Monte Darwin and three other peaks. Though other expeditions have visited the range since that date, most of its peaks still remain unclimbed.

II ACCESS TO AREAS NORTH OF LAT. 46°S.

The Cordillera Darwin can only be reached by sea. Punta Arenas is the most convenient port of approach. It should be possible, with plenty of notice, to hire vessels from there. Ships of the Chilean navy plying between Punta Arenas and the Beagle Channel take passengers by special arrangement. Permission of the naval authorities is needed to visit the area.

The southern end of the Patagonian Andes, including the Paines group, is best approached by road from Punta Arenas. Lorries can be hired.

The region west of Lago Argentino is the most

Opposite: Head of Bahia Broken, Tierra del Fuego.

Mt Darwin from the head of the Marinelli Glacier, 8,700 ft.

easily accessible. There is a regular civil air service between Buenos Aires and El Calafate, where there are several stores selling food, etc., and the National Parks administration runs a launch on the lake.

Lagos Viedma and San Martin can be approached by air to Santa Cruz and thence by lorry. There is a launch of sorts on the latter, but it is unreliable. The farms near the foot of FitzRoy (Lago Viedma) can be reached by road.

There are regular flights to an airfield at the eastern end of Lago Buenos Aires whence the Rio Baker can be reached by government launch. From there Monte San Lorenzo can be reached by pack transport. There are considerable physical difficulties involved in the eastern approaches to the Hielo Patagonico del Norte, and this region can best be reached by launch (hired locally) from Puerto Aisen to Laguna San Rafael, and thence up the San Rafael Glacier. Even this is not easy.

The western approach to any part of the Patagonian Andes can only be made by sea.

It would, of course, be possible to reach most parts of the range by helicopter or by light ski- or float-aircraft, but these means would be very costly and, in the weather conditions normally prevailing, unreliable.

Opposite: North Ridge of Cerro Yaghan, a peak in the Darwin Range named by Shipton after an extinct Indian tribe.

Overleaf: Towers of Paine.

The distant hills

Chapter 6

Technique

With the advent of 'artificial' climbing the whole conception of difficulty has undergone a radical change: there are virtually no routes today which cannot be climbed – given the right party, clothing and equipment

ARTIFICIAL AIDS *John Longland*

Artificial aids are probably as old as climbing itself – they were used to assist the first ascent of Mont Aiguille by de Ville in 1492! Since then they have had a chequered history: used by the alpine pioneers; later almost a guarantee of exclusion from the Alpine Club (on the grounds that their use was unsporting); more recently used on the highest mountain in the world.

What then is an artificial aid? Curiously, it is closer to the layman's picture of climbing than most climbers are prepared to admit. An artificial aid is a piece of equipment that enables climbing progress to be made beyond a point where any unequipped climber would be forced to turn back. They therefore exclude boots, probably include portable oxygen-set environments, and certainly embrace anything attached to a mountain in lieu of an absent natural hand or foothold.

The simplest form of artificial aid is the *piton*, which is a spike with a hole at one end, that can be hammered into ice or a crack in rock. *Indirectly* a piton can be used to provide safety, by attaching a party to a mountain in the absence of a natural belay, and thus lessen the risk of a major accident; *directly* it can provide the missing hand or foothold. Direct or indirect, the equipment is the same. Pitons come in a great range of shapes and sizes to fit different situations. Recent research has shown most European pitons to have low holding power, and now American design and metallurgy lead the field.

Used for direct aid, a piton alone is an unfriendly object, with a hole only large enough for

Opposite: Artificial aids on Swanage sea-cliff.

Overleaf: Glen Denny leading the Great Roof on El Capitan.

Steve Roper waiting to haul loads on the Nose of El Capitan.

a finger. Given a stirrup clipped to it by a snaplink a climber can sit in comfort, and with a hammock he can spend the night. Stirrups, or *étriers*, used to be made just like two- or three-rung rope ladders, but now have evolved into loops of nylon tape which are kinder on the underside of the thigh and do not tangle so easily.

All this is fine. Select a smooth, even overhanging, wall of rock split by a crack; hammer in a piton; clip on an étrier; climb up the étrier; hammer in the next piton; and so on until the top. If the crack is wide, hammer in a wooden wedge; if the wall is ice, turn in a piton like a household corkscrew. Simple, though surprisingly energetic.

But what happens when there is no convenient crack up the smooth rock? Again American

Layton Korr and Steve Roper.

invention comes to the rescue, with equipment developed in the artificial mecca of the Yosemite Valley. The first aid is the *skyhook*. This small metal hook can hang on a minute flake or bubble of rock that no hand could ever hold, and then is used precisely like a piton. Secondly, the climber can use an *expansion bolt*. Evolved from the household masonry bolt, this needs a hole to be drilled (a long, tedious and tiring business), a soft metal sleeve and a threaded piton.

Given this armoury and bearable conditions, clearly any mountain problem must yield to a siege. However there are snags. Even with the latest materials the equipment can weigh a lot. A leading climber can only perform with a limited load, so he must judge the necessities finely and his follower must retrieve all possible equipment for the next ropelength. Removing artificial aids is often more demanding than placing them. Because of this, on classical routes, the climber can expect to find the pitons in place on a permanent basis and be saved taking the equipment of the pioneer.

For perspective, it must be said that many climbers have never used an artificial aid. Most mountains can be climbed without them, but given a magnificent virgin route with a few apparently 'impossible' feet, what pioneer can resist the temptation to discover what the mountain is like just a little bit farther up?

Hardware used on South Buttress of El Capitan.

Opposite far left: Chuck Pratt.
Opposite left: Claude Barbier who soloed all three North Faces of the Lavaredo in 6½ hours.

Modern ice climbing equipment in use on The Ramp, Matterhorn North Face.

MODERN MOUNTAIN CLOTHING AND EQUIPMENT

Ian Clough

No survey of contemporary mountaineering would be complete without giving consideration to the material aids which assist the modern climber. Since the pioneering days of Norfolk jackets, hobnail boots and hemp ropes a great change has been brought about in mountain clothing and equipment, increasing comfort, safety and survival-potential and consequently leading to much bolder psychological attitudes.

It was only in relatively recent years that it was realised that mountaineering required specialised designs and materials. For many years discarded day-to-day clothing was deemed suitable, with the addition perhaps of an anorak, a garment which was, at best, wind and showerproof. In heavy rain one became wet; an extra sweater was the answer in extreme cold.

Modern designing and new materials have produced clothing which not only conserves heat far more efficiently and totally excludes wind and water, but is also far lighter in weight. Modern equipment is subtly, scientifically, thought-out; is stronger, lighter and more durable.

Footwear (now almost exclusively rubber soled) comes in many specialised forms, from the super lightweight rock boot to high altitude boots which, whilst remaining neat, incorporate a felt inner for warmth. Net or string underwear provides ventilation next to the skin and prevents insulating garments from becoming moist and inefficient through perspiration. Down has proved over several years to be an excellent insulating agent for conditions of extreme cold. It is so light and compressable that a down-filled

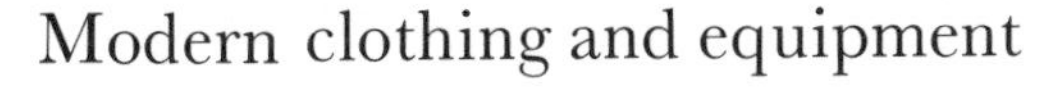

By way of contrast – equipment used by Whymper in 1865.

jacket and short sleeping bag can be conveniently carried in one's rucksack even if a bivouac is not contemplated. A recent innovation in the insulation field are garments utilising nylon fibre pile. Stockings based on this principle have already proved very effective.

The relatively recent introduction of strong ultra-light-weight nylon-based materials which provide complete protection against wind and water has revolutionised mountaineering clothing. It is commonly used as an outer layer for bad weather conditions in the form of the cagoule (a knee-length hooded smock) and overtrousers. Bivouac sacs made of the same material and weighing only a few ounces provide an emergency shelter in which it is possible to survive several days of storm.

The use of nylon has also greatly improved the properties of climbing ropes. Old fashioned hemp ropes had many disadvantages and provided little real safeguard for the first man on the rope. Modern ropes are lightweight, strong enough to withstand incredibly severe loadings and yet have considerable elasticity, thus reducing the possibility of a falling leader suffering internal injuries.

The modern climbing leader uses many and various accessories to safeguard his advance. Slings of nylon rope (or tape), hung over rock spikes (or threaded behind jammed stones) and connected to the main rope by metal snap-links or karabiners, provide the most basic form of running belay, reducing the distance of the leader's potential fall. Modern 'protection' involves the use of numerous slings and karabiners in conjunction with nuts (which are jammed in crack constrictions), pegs and even expansion bolts (metal spikes driven into cracks or into a drilled hole). The modern leader is almost invulnerable to the consequences of a fall, particularly since the recent general acceptance of protective helmets of plastic or fibreglass.

Nowadays a single rucksack can contain all the necessities for several days' combat with the most severe technical problems and weather conditions that mountains can provide. The modern climber can afford to be considerably bolder than his predecessors; his superb equipment is his safeguard as he reduces the bounds of impossibility.

Chapter 7

The Anatomy of the Hills

Of crucial importance to the mountaineer is the nature of the rock – and ice and snow – on which he climbs

THE ROCK ON WHICH WE CLIMB *N.E. Odell*

The three big groups of rocks are (*a*) the igneous, eruptive or so-called 'fire-formed' rocks, cooled from an originally molten condition, like granite, gabbro and basalt; (*b*) the sedimentary rocks, usually in layered formations, e.g. limestones, sandstones and shales; and (*c*), the altered or metamorphic kinds of rock, which are derived sometimes from group (*a*) and sometimes from group (*b*), giving rise to types such as slate or marble, schist or gneiss. Geology studies the origin of these various rocks, but all we need say here is that those in group (*a*) were intruded hot from below, deep or shallow within pre-existing formations, or poured out at the surface to form volcanoes, lava-flows or beds of so-called ash (tuff); (*b*) were laid down in water, or under the agency of wind; whereas group (*c*) attained their altered condition from the effects of changing temperature, or of pressure in the earth's crust.

Nature of the rocks. All these rocks can vary widely in their characters of roughness, toughness and structure from the point of view of climbing; and then of the greatest importance is the kind of wearing down (denudation) that through long ages they may have suffered, whether from the effects of weathering, of water, or of snow and ice. As to the igneous rocks, everyone knows of the general character of granite, usually light in colour, with its 'acid' composition, and its rough crystalline texture, due mainly to quartz, felspar and mica crystals; also how it (or its near relative, grano-diorite) forms not infrequently the core of mountain ranges: e.g. parts of the Alps,

Opposite: From the Säntis: rocks in the near and middle distance are limestone of the 'Säntis Nappe' of the High Calcareous Alps: the region is waterless, all water having percolated through the limestone.

Matterhorn summit, itself of Valpelline gneisses; Monte Rosa and mountains in right background are portions of the 'Monte Rosa Nappe' composed chiefly of gneisses of both sedimentary and igneous origin.

such as the Mont Blanc range; portions of the inner Himalayas; the great Coast range, B.C.; and the Sierra Nevada, California. But equal, or even better, in these qualities of roughness and toughness is the dark 'basic' rock, gabbro, so preeminent in the Cuillin hills of Skye or the pinnacles of the Lofoten islands and elsewhere. Yet under some climatic conditions granite and even gabbro can become weathered and very unstable and rotten. Their essential felspar crystals decompose, and the resistant quartz crystals (in the case of granite), deprived of their cementing minerals, tend to crumble and fall away. As to basalt and allied types, although intrinsically hard black rocks, and often tough, yet their steep cliffs can at times be very treacherous to the climber. This can frequently be detected by a change of colour, especially along cracks and joints, where weathering and decomposition may be taking place.

In the case of sedimentary formations, we have a great range of rocks, varying enormously in substance, durability and indeed landscape form. These are the sandstones, often relatively soft or disintegrating, yet sometimes solid and gritty, e.g. gritstone of northern England etc. Again, the limestones, giving steep cliffs with cracks and joints, are frequently friable and treacherous; there is, on the other hand, the dolomite variety of limestone, that is usually tough and resistant to weathering. The Dolomite range of Tyrol is in part an example (but see below). Shales and slates also can greatly vary in their consistency, but are usually of poor climbing quality. With

Opposite: On the Kingspitz, Engelhörner: steeply dipping hard limestone strata of the 'Morcles Nappe', extending eastwards from the Dents de Morcles.

Overleaf: Banff National Park, peaks left to right: Mt Lefroy (11,230 ft) Big Beehive (middle foreground) Mt Victoria (11,365 ft) and Mt Whyte (9,786 ft). All rocks are of Cambrian age chiefly quartzites (metamorphosed sandstones) with some inter-bedded shales.

On the Gletschhorn – probably granite of the Aar Massif.

This glacier heads up through the 'Death Trap' to Abbot Pass with the cliffs of Mt Victoria on the right and those of Mt Lefroy on the left. Rocks predominantly quartzite of Cambrian age.

the above can be grouped the 'fragmental' deposits: sediments such as sands, clays and gravels, which have been derived from the waste of preexisting rocks, and later become consolidated into conglomerates (with rounded pebbles) and breccias (with angular particles). Such rocks are found inter-bedded in many composite formations, but can occur on a massive scale in some areas, as for instance in the Bakhtiari ranges of south Persia. The Torridon mountains of Scotland are in part conglomerate though mainly of sandstone. It is of great interest that even the topmost rocks of Mount Everest have been found to be of sedimentary marine origin (platy limestone and calc-schist), and lately (1963) have been shown by Professor A. Gansser, of Zürich, to contain tiny fragments of fossils.

The altered rocks. Metamorphic rocks cover as wide a range in actual composition as they do in making up so much of the materials of so many major mountain ranges. But whether slate or marble (recrystallised limestone), schist or gneiss – as perhaps chief representatives of these 'altered' rocks – they nearly always have one characteristic in common and that is cleavage and/or foliation. Slaty cleavage is a structure developed by compressional and shearing forces acting within the crust of the earth during certain mountain-building movements. It can frequently bear no relationship to the original bedding planes of the rock, and may cut across it at all angles. If well-developed, together with bedding and jointing, it can have a marked effect on the weathering of the rock. Allied to cleavage in certain metamorphic rocks is foliation, due to the parallel disposition in layers or lines or lenses of one or more of the conspicuous minerals. Foliation is to be seen in gneisses of various kinds, sometimes on a finer scale, and at other times coarser, when it is known as 'banding'. Related to foliation, though not necessarily coincident with it, is schistosity (cleavage), characteristic in schists of very many kinds. It is a property of a foliated rock whereby it can be divided into thin flakes or lenticles, and is developed *par excellence* in the well-known mica-schists. But as opposed to the banded and streaky character of the above metamorphic rocks we have in pure marble (recrystallised limestone) a more massive appearance and consistency, and one usually of fine-grained texture. But less pure marble can have the well-known variegated colours (e.g. Carrara marble); and if magnesia is present it becomes a dolomite marble. Incidentally, the Dolomite range of the eastern Alps is not entirely composed of dolomite, but contains much pure limestone, and in some areas a mixture of the two. Much discussion has in the past taken place about the origin of these particular vast limestone deposits, which were thought to be due to the formation of ancient coral reefs and atolls; but as the late mountaineer, Professor Garwood, has stated in the Lonsdale volume of *Mountaineering*, many of the beds have been found to be the result of deposition of lime from sea-water during the growth of humble plants of the calcareous algae kind. Another 'massive' rock in this class is quartzite, which is sandstone crystallised and cemented under high pressure, and which often contributes to the composition of sedimentary formations in mountain ranges. Quartzite must, incidentally, be carefully distinguished from quartz itself, which is frequently present in veins and/or other irregular masses, having originally been injected as hot solutions, or secreted in the process of metamorphism. But such 'massive' sedimentary rocks as those cited above are apt to be fractured or shattered by the effects of movement or weathering, and they are not always reliable from the point of view of climbing.

Structure of formations in general. Such well-known characters as the dip, or inclination, of the formations should be self-evident to all climbers. Moreover, inward-dipping strata, rather than outward-dipping, is always an important factor in assessing the advantages of an ascent of one flank or another of a mountain. Horizontally lying beds in a crag can vary greatly in the quality of their 'free' climbing. This necessarily depends on the actual composition of the rock and its degree of weathering along certain beds. Then, during compression and movement in the earth's crust, fractures yielding faults of various kinds may develop. In the case of the related phenomenon of jointing, there will be no evidence of movement of rock on rock, but through the action of weathering, joints can become gaping features traversing the formations often in more than one direction; vertically, horizontally and perhaps otherwise, and sometimes giving rise to steep inaccessible walls, and often to blocky mountain peaks. Faults define notable lines or zones of movement, and they can have profound effects at times on the dispositions of local formations, but usually not such as to impede the climber.

Weathering. As a geological process, weathering is of two kinds: (1) physical (or mechanical), due to temperature changes, such as heat-expansion or frost-action; and (2) chemical, resulting in

Opposite: Near Bujuku Lake, Alexandra and Margherita Peaks with giant groundsels in the foreground.
Overleaf: K2 from Concordia – 15 miles to the south.

mineral decomposition in the rock. Physical weathering produces one of the most powerful effects in shattering rock, and in the tropical and sub-tropical zones the effect on granite surfaces particularly is to cause them to spall off (exfoliate), on account of differential expansion of the constituent minerals through rapid heating: the 'inselbergs' of South Africa and the walls and summits of the Yosemite valley, California, are spectacular examples. On the other hand, rapid cooling, particularly at night, in the rocks of high mountains, and in many desert areas, causes contraction and the development of cracks which may become joints in the mass of the rock. Into these cracks will percolate water from melting snow during day-time, especially in the case of high mountains, followed by nightly freezing. This frost-action can exert tremendous pressures within the rocks: up to 2,000 lbs per sq in.

In the case of chemical weathering, it is mineral decomposition that is the prime cause of disintegration. Rain or other water acts as a carrier of dissolved oxygen and carbon dioxide, plus various acids or organic products that may be derived from the soil. Only a few common rock-minerals resist chemical decomposition, and these are principally quartz and white mica (muscovite and sericite). The chief changes, then, are oxidation and carbonation, where in the case of the latter process rock carbonates are vigorously attacked in the presence of carbon dioxide and may go entirely into solution, so that whole limestone ranges become honeycombed with channels, caves and pot-holes to provide for many climbers and others the allied pursuit of speleology.

In general it can be said that the eruptive (igneous) rocks are more susceptible to weathering than the sedimentary, with the exception of limestone and other calcareous varieties. This is because sedimentary rocks are the accumulated débris or detrital remains of the eruptives which have been already decomposed. Moreover, the 'basic' eruptives (e.g. basalt, dolerite etc.) are more readily attacked than the 'acid' kinds (e.g. granite, syenite, etc.), owing to the larger proportion of chemical bases in them. The (petrological) basic varieties, therefore, tend to form depressions or gullies, while the (petrological) acid rocks will often stand out as ridges or summits in the landscape.

Finally, the resulting progressive shattering and disintegration of rock of whatever kind will often produce the great slopes of talus or scree, which are such a feature of many mountain ranges, becoming the bane of the ascending climber, though often a delight for his quick descent.

Opposite above: Alexandra and Margherita Peaks on Mt Stanley.
Opposite below: The Savoia Peak on Mt Stanley.

Overleaf: Typical pure dolomite rock, horizontally bedded and vertically jointed – Lavaredo.

Conditions promising – for the skier – much joy in deep powder snow free of wind-pack.

Glacier-dammed lake: Märjelensee.

SNOW, ICE AND GLACIERS *André Roch*

Mountains may be beautiful simply because of their upthrusting outlines, but when clad with snow and glaciers they become even more spectacular and impressive. These adornments of snow and ice have compelled alpinists to develop special techniques and equipment for climbing on them. The ferruled stick was replaced by a large ice-axe, then by a smaller axe, which ultimately became the handy multi-purpose ice-axe of today. The nailing of climbing boots was steadily improved and then replaced by crampons, which are now light and adjustable for all boot sizes.

Some knowledge of snow and ice may be useful to the alpinist and contribute to sound reasoning when choosing a route or making a decision during a climb. And this knowledge helps to develop an appreciation of conditions and dangers in the mountains – an appreciation that the old guides only acquired through experience, observation and instinct.

Snow has varied properties: it may be as light as featherdown, as viscous as honey, or as hard as concrete. It begins life in the atmosphere as the result of the sublimation of water vapour, or by the crystallisation of supercooled water droplets, around nuclei which may be tiny particles of either dust or ice.

In this way, according to conditions of temperature and supersaturation of humidity in the atmosphere, one or other of the many wondrous forms of ice crystal is created. They may be needles, hexagonal plates, six-pointed stars, columns, columns capped by end plates or stars,

Star with central plate.

spatial forms, and so on. As soon as they are sufficiently heavy they are precipitated, falling either simply or as flakes made up of several crystals that aggregate during their earthward journey.

The meteorological conditions throughout their fall influence the type of snow once on the ground. In windstill, low-temperature conditions, the crystals accumulate in a very light snow layer. If the temperature is higher, the crystals are softer, their branches are more malleable, and the snow layer settles and becomes compact. Above 0 °C, melt-water makes the snow sticky and rotten.

Wind during the snow-fall breaks and rolls the crystals, which then agglomerate into a compact layer. This layer is of irregular thickness because the windward slopes are swept almost bare and the snow accumulates in sheltered areas. The wind forms cornices on the ridges, and snow-shields and drifts on the slopes.

Once on the ground, the original snow crystals change their shape continuously, and the higher the temperature the more rapid these changes. The fine points of the needles and stars tend to disappear, for their ice sublimes into water vapour which then moves towards the central and thicker parts of the crystals where it recondenses. The original branching crystals thus become grains, fine at first and then larger.

And within the snow layers, the crystals may undergo another sort of transformation. It is relatively warm deep in the snow cover, whereas the upper layers are colder because they are affected by the low temperatures of winter, and high-altitude nights. Owing to these temperature differences, the air in the pores of the snow cover may rise through the layers, become cooled, then supersaturated, and deposit its moisture on certain crystals that are favourably oriented. These crystals grow and take on the form of prisms and little cups, while other crystals that are giving off water vapour lower in the snow cover disappear. (These cup crystals can attain a length of 3–4 mm in the snow cover and 40–50 mm in crevasses or ice caves.) In this way, snow layers may gradually be transformed into a scaffolding of small conical cup crystals that have very weak points of contact between them. Such layers are very fragile and may sometimes bridge large crevasses. They break very easily under the weight of an alpinist. Long cold periods are favourable for the formation of this so-called depth hoar.

Following a heavy fall of new snow, the lower layers of the snow cover compress under the additional weight and become compact. On the other hand, the crystals of a snow layer that has remained for a long period on the surface without melting become granular, lose their compressibility and will continue to constitute a loose, light and friable layer even when covered by other strata.

In winter, at high altitude, snow hardly adheres to ridges and abrupt faces, for it is generally blown clear. The crystals roll and tumble to the bottom of the slopes where they accumulate.

It is only at the end of spring, in May, June and during the summer, that snow falling on steep slopes – after rain or a warm day, for example – sticks to them and so covers slopes that have remained as blue ice all winter.

But snow crystals do have other means, apart from thawing and re-freezing, for adhering to steep faces. The stars and needles of new snow interlock among themselves and achieve a felt-like cohesion which may enable them to cling even to vertical surfaces. Thus, rock faces become

Mer de Glace.

snow-plastered, though high winds may later tear snow from the rocks and swirl it like seagulls into the sky. The sun warms the rock through the slabs of snow still in place and certain of them come unstuck and fall; the rest freeze to the face.

In summer, melt-water trickles down the gulleys and couloirs. At night it freezes in the cracks in the rock and also in the crevasses of glaciers. Since ice has a larger volume than water, the freezing melt-water produces an expansion force which may split the rock or glacier. It can happen that stones unseated by this expansion of freezing melt-water may still be held in place by the ice, and will only be released by the sun's rays as they thaw that ice. One must therefore fear ice and stonefalls when it is cold at night and when the day's heat is sufficient to cause a thaw on the faces thus releasing them.

By thawing during the day and refreezing at night, the snow gradually becomes névé. The crystals grow with the melt-water which freezes to them. They become rounded, freeze one to another and form snow which is hard and compact – excellent for glacier climbing. But occasionally only the top layer of snow on a slope melts and refreezes, and it then constitutes a hard surface on underlying strata of rotten snow. Such a situation may be unstable and dangerous.

At certain altitudes (between 4,500 metres and 5,500 metres in the Himalayas), the solar radiation is intense but the air temperature is relatively low. The effect of the sun's radiation is concentrated into the hollows that are protected from the cold air currents. These hollows are then deepened by the effect of melting while the hummocks remain. This process finally produces snow columns standing proud of the general surface, and these columns gradually change to ice. They may attain 10 metres in height. (Khumbu Glacier, Everest.)

In the Alps, similar formations, from 30–40 cms high, sometimes appear on south slopes in February and March. They are called penitents of snow and ice, a name which comes from the Andes ('nieve penitentes').

Above 6,500 metres in the Himalayas, the snow never melts except close to rocks heated by the sun. The melt-water evaporates into the very dry air of such altitudes. It is in this way that holes and caverns form on ridges that are made up of part rock and part snow. Combined with cornices, these conditions make progress along the ridge both delicate and dangerous.

On large glaciers at these altitudes, the snow is a sort of flour in which walking is tiresome, but once disturbed by the passing of a climbing party, this snow hardens and progress is easier. One should, therefore, always mark the track from one camp to another so as to be able to refind the firm base after a blizzard.

The gigantic organ-pipes on the steep snow slopes of the Andes and Himalayas form progressively. Each snowfall that occurs during fairly calm conditions covers the mountains uniformly. The warmth of the sun loosens wedges of snow that sweep down the furrows while the snow on the ridges remains, settles and hardens. In this way, the accumulations on the ridges grow while the furrows are regularly swept clean.

At high altitude where the year's snowfall does not melt entirely, successive layers build up on gentle slopes and especially at the foot of rock faces from which it has slid down. There is therefore a permanent snow cover. By melting and refreezing, and under the weight of successive layers, this snow gradually changes to ice, which then flows towards the valleys forming magnificent glaciers.

The catchment area that feeds the upper part of the glacier is covered by névé, to which another layer is added each year. In addition, avalanches fall from the slopes and faces of the catchment area and this accumulation helps to feed the glacier. The thickness of the snow/ice cover in these areas does not increase indefinitely because the mass flows away downhill. Below the permanent snow line, the tongue of the glacier, which melts to a certain extent each summer, subsists owing to the ice carried from above. If this transport of ice exactly compensates ablation, the glacier is in a state of balance. If not, the thickness and length of the tongue will diminish. If, on the other hand, the mass carried by the flow is in excess of that eliminated by ablation, the glacier will advance. At Chamonix, the Glacier des Bossons, which descends lower than any other in the Alps, advances at a rate of 1·5 metres a day. The large Aletsch Glacier advances 10 cms a day at the Jungfraujoch, and 70 cms a day in front of the Concordia hut. These speeds are, of course, variable.

As a result of a slight rise in average air temperatures over the last fifty years glaciers were generally retreating throughout the world. But in very recent years in the Alps the number of glaciers that are growing (once only four or five in Switzerland) is now increasing and exceeds one third of the 110 glaciers under observation.

The ice of glaciers is formed of crystals of agglomerated snow, which has melted, refrozen, and compressed. At the beginning, this ice contains a high proportion of air. Some of this

Opposite: West Face, Döme du Goûter.

air escapes as the ice compacts, but some remains enclosed in the mass, and these air bubbles become compressed. Under the effect of the continual thrust of the glacier, the ice particles grow. At the end of a very long glacier, they may be fist-sized or even bigger.

The sun's radiation tends to part the ice crystals near the surface. The glacier climber must know of this phenomenon, for an ice bollard, cut to place a rope rappel, may suddenly disintegrate. Similarly, when driving an ice piton, it is as well to remove the top surface of the ice with an axe or hammer and embed the piton in the more compact ice exposed in the bottom of the niche so formed.

Snow slopes are hardly ever steeper than 60°, for snow will not hold on steeper inclines, unless in gullies – where it is supported on both sides – or in cracks. On slopes of 45° to 50°, the slightest obstacles hold the snow, and avalanches feed what are called hanging glaciers. These are masses of ice adhering to slopes, and from below they present impressive blue-green fracture lines. These ice masses flow slowly and sometimes slabs detach themselves and fall with a thunderous roar. The thickness of hanging glaciers depends on the plasticity of the flowing ice. In temperate zones they may reach a thickness of 100 metres, but they are thicker in the polar regions where the ambient air temperature is lower and makes the ice less plastic. The mass of these hanging glaciers varies. For tens of years they may make certain faces inaccessible to climbers, and then they disappear, probably having fallen as an ice avalanche. A few years later they have reformed. An example of this phenomenon occurs on the north face of the Aiguille d'Argentière which dominates the Saleinaz Glacier in the Swiss part of the Mont Blanc chain.

When a thick glacier flows on a slope steeper than 20°, the ice becomes crevassed in all directions and large blocks and towers are formed. These are called seracs; they sometimes topple and set others in motion to form an ice avalanche. In an area of seracs, the glacier surface is so chaotic that it may be very difficult to climb.

Below these frozen cascades, the ice river regains its normal course. The surface is marked by dark diagonal ribs which succeed each other year after year. These are accumulations of debris that have been deformed by glacier movement. They are called Forbes' bands after the Scottish naturalist and alpinist who first described them.

Along the edges of the ice river, the flow is slowed against the rocks and this forms many lateral crevasses.

At the foot of steep snow or ice slopes dominating a glacier, one or two cracks demarcate the edge of the ice or of the snow on the slope and the moving ice of the glacier. These crevasses are called rimayes. After each snowfall, avalanches, or simply snow crystals rolling to the bottom of the steep slope, tend to fill the rimaye; but it re-opens regularly.

The most dangerous glaciers are those lying on dome-shaped humps, cols, or glacial plateaux. They flow down on all sides and split in every direction. Generally, their crevasses are hidden by windblown snow.

Thick glaciers on slopes steeper than 10° split a great deal, and snowfalls cover the crevasses. In the convex parts of the slope, the cracks continue to widen at the top, which stretches the snow bridges until they become very fragile. And the transformation of the snow cover into a scaffolding of cup crystals (depth hoar) also makes snow bridges fragile. In sum, whenever a glacier becomes snow-covered, it is dangerous because the crevasses are hidden.

The stones which fall from the flanking slopes of a glacier are carried down and form lateral moraines. These trace the movement of the ice in a most remarkable way.

At the junction of two glaciers, the lateral moraines join to form a medial moraine. The stones transported and left at the lower extremity of a glacier are the frontal moraine.

Under the glacier, the rock is polished and striated by the stones dragged along under the ice. These are the rounded rocks visible when a glacier retreats, called 'rockes moutonnees'.

The study of glaciers is a science that is in full development, and sometimes alpinists contribute to it almost unintentionally.

Climbing on glaciers is not more difficult than climbing on rock, but since the material on which one is climbing is very varied, such ascents do call for greater experience. One is exposed to additional dangers, but these climbs do have one reassuring aspect, remarked upon by Maurice Crettex, a famous guide from Champex, 'Wherever there is snow, one can go!'

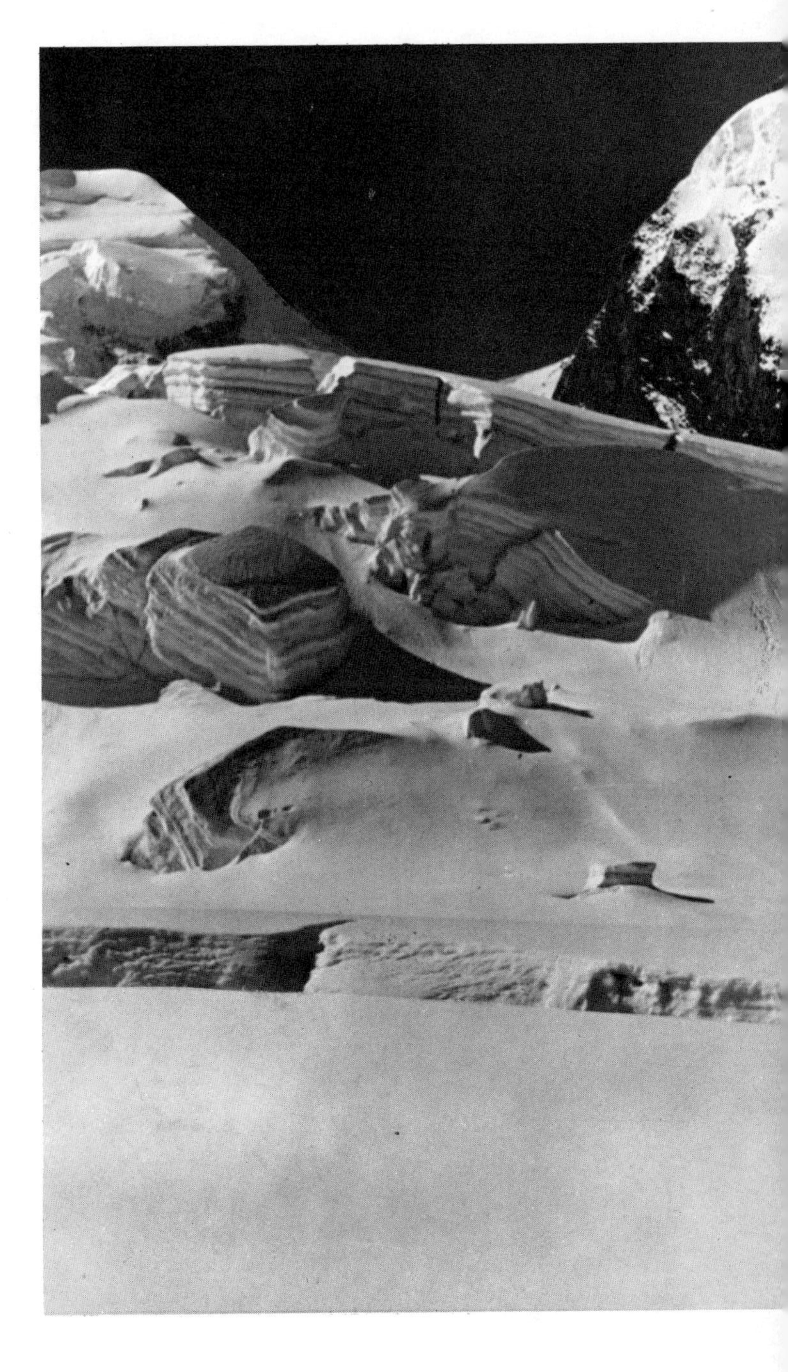

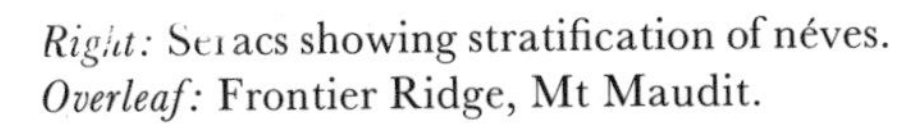

Right: Seracs showing stratification of néves.
Overleaf: Frontier Ridge, Mt Maudit.

Chapter 8

The Woman Climber

In climbing, just as in skiing, the top women cannot compete on equal terms with the best men but nevertheless their recent performances in both spheres have been highly meritorious. Monica Jackson, who has a list of routes to her credit of which most men would be proud, reviews the part that women play in the contemporary mountain world

Monica Jackson

A discussion of the role played by women in modern mountaineering, if confined to a single chapter, must necessarily stick to generalisations. It will therefore be impossible here, sad to say, to enumerate individual exploits and successes except in certain instances where they serve as examples of tendencies and trends.

We are all very much aware of subjective barriers in the climbing world. Everest, the Eigerwand or Cenotaph Corner, once climbed and seen to be possible, is climbed again and again with decreasing difficulty. Of course the principle is a general one and operates so universally that it could almost be described as a natural law, but in this case we have to consider it specifically in relation to climbing and particularly to women climbing. The psychological barriers to women's full participation in climbing as a sport have been formidable.

With the exception of isolated communities such as the Malayalams of Kerala and even – to some extent – the Sherpas of Nepal, the last time the female sex as a whole was regarded by the community as at least the equal of the male in ability was a very long time ago, before the barbarian tribes of the north with their male gods conquered the ancient civilisations of the Mediterranean and Asia Minor who worshipped the 'mother' or the 'lady', the goddess of regeneration whose inspiration survives in reverence for the Mother of God. It may seem somewhat far-fetched, as well as rather funny, to suggest that concepts about the sex of the deity can have any bearing on human activity in such a comparatively

Monica Jackson and Jill Goldsmith in Turkish Khurdistan.

minor and limited field as mountaineering, but it does have a certain relevance in its effects on traditional outlooks. Climbing, for instance, like riding and sailing, but unlike athletics and most competitive ball games, appears to be a sport in which women can participate on equal terms with men. A woman's balance is as good as man's, as a visit to the circus will confirm. She has as much courage, and more endurance because she is biologically built to survive. On snow and ice, at high altitudes and on long routes she is just as likely to do well. It is true that the lack of muscular development in her arms and fingers may seem to preclude vertical or overhanging rock climbs of the severest category, but women now lead on very hard rock climbs and follow up even harder. (I am not speaking of those who allow themselves to be dragged up, who fall into the same category as those men and women who allow themselves to be dangled by guides on the Matterhorn so as to say they have done it – 'c'est magnifique, peut-etre, mais ce n'est pas la varappe'.) Of course there are still a good many rock routes, reckoned to be within the compass of the best male climbers, which the top female climbers have not yet got around to considering from the point of view of leading them. This is what one of our best woman rock climbers has called 'the rock ceiling', and does not necessarily mean that women cannot lead them but that the margin of safety in so doing, because of their lesser physical strength, may make the attempt unjustifiable. Nevertheless the rock ceiling for women is still being pushed up.

Why then, if women have proved themselves to be physically capable of doing hard climbs, have they shown less initiative in this sport than men have? This, I believe, is where the psychological barrier comes in. Furthermore on closer inspection two barriers are revealed. The first may be termed social. It is still true that there is something about a woman taking up mountaineering, which admittedly tends to be a way of life as much as a sport, that seems to surprise and even to offend many non-climbers. There is a vague impression that there is something unnatural about it, whereas it is simply a phenomenon of the modern world and limited to an affluent society, as indeed is the whole cult of mountaineering. (Those whose lives are normally spent in a struggle for survival don't go climbing mountains by choice. In the same way it is only when freed from the burdens of excessive child-bearing and drudgery that an increasing number of western women have energy to spare and the leisure and independence to use it as they wish.) But the myth persists that women who mountaineer seriously must be over-masculine or sexually frustrated, and this in spite of the fact that a large percentage of us are wives and mothers, that with few exceptions the unmarried ones are equally feminine and have equally satisfying careers, and that some of our best climbers are charming girls with all the suitors anyone could wish.

It has yet to be completely accepted that mountaineering can have as great an aesthetic and romantic attraction for women as for men and that they may derive as much satisfaction as men do from the sense of adventure and achievement which it provides. Admittedly non-climbers are as a rule more disapproving than the climbing world, but there is still a good deal of remarkably reactionary suspicion of woman mountaineers floating around among male climbers, which makes any breakthrough by the women considerably more difficult. As recently as 1961 when a woman friend and I went to climb the Matterhorn – by the Hörnli ridge, for goodness sake! – we were greeted at the Belvedere with the words: 'You're mad. Go back to Zermatt,' because we were guideless. Certainly the conditions were poor (or we'd have been doing something more enterprising), but whereas we were quietly minding our own business, the sour looks and comments of the guides we encountered on the ascent were calculated to make us feel we were committing some vulgar indiscretion by proceeding to the summit. Imagine then the pressure of dissident opinion when a *cordée féminine* sets out to do a hard climb.

The second barrier may be called an intrinsic or functional one. On the whole women are far less aggressive than men. This is of course a truly sweeping generalisation, since there are plenty of aggressive and competitive females about, but it is justified by the statistics of both driving and crime. The corollary is that as mountaineers they tend to be less enterprising and single-minded in their objectives and ambitions, and these attributes are essential for the planning and achievement of hard climbs. On the credit side it may be said that the built-in female inclination towards conservation rather than wastage of life may make for safety and reliability in the experienced woman climber. And if the unkind observation may be forgiven, any tendency to diffusion of interests will be warmly welcomed by those who have been compelled to spend an evening with a climbing bore.

So much for intangible problems. Among the practical ones it is obvious that the tie of children

Opposite: Barbara Spark and Duggie Baines on Mur Y Niwl, Craig Yr Ysfa.

is the most intractable of solution.

The history of women's climbing reveals some interesting trends. Beginning predictably with the few pioneering personalities, mostly British, who were drawn to the heights regardless of inconvenient garments and the conventional view that ladies were delicate creatures and who climbed with male relatives and guides, we come to the age between the wars when a number of financially 'comfortable' women were climbing regularly with some of the best alpine guides and doing many of the greatest routes. At the same time women were beginning to climb seriously with male relatives and friends on British cliffs and with each other under the auspices of female clubs such as the Pinnacle and Ladies Scottish Climbing Club. In the thirties female climbing received a great impetus through the exploits of people like Nea Morin, Miriam Underhill and others who, from climbing hard routes at home and abroad with their husbands, moved on to guideless *cordée féminine* rock climbing of a serious order in the Alps and Dolomites. By the thirties and forties Swiss and French women, like the redoubtable Loulou Boulaz, were also doing remarkable alpine climbs, though nearly always with men, and in Britain experts like Nea Morin and Brenda Ritchie were leading some of the most sensational climbs then listed. The fifties, which saw a great expansion, almost a revolution, in the climbing world, also saw unconcerned acceptance in Britain of the female climbing team on climbs of high standard. But not, strangely enough, on the Continent, where women climbers of equal or greater ability, however steely their nerves and fingers, still seemed to prefer male company and moral support on the big routes. The fifties also saw the first female teams in the Himalayas – another British innovation.

In the late sixties the graph of women's climbing has reached a plateau. This is not to say there has been no progress. On the contrary, the spectacle in Britain of young women climbing and often leading the hardest climbs in the country has become such a commonplace that it is difficult to find out what has and has not been done. On the Continent, too, women are doing routes of extreme severity, and here again, because they are doing them for their own satisfaction and not to prove anything to the world at large, no records are kept. But the point is that these women in Western Europe nearly always climb with men. As respected partners no doubt, but it is hard to say how much they may rely on masculine physical strength on the more strenuous pitches. It is surprising how the *cordée féminine* is still a matter for comment and even raised eyebrows in the Alps. In 1962 two young women, Faye Kerr and Dorothée Borys, completed – guideless and for their own amusement – a number of classic alpine traverses. They were astonished to find that they created quite a stir and that in some cases, such as the north ridge on the Weisshorn and the Zmutt on the Matterhorn, these turned out to be *cordée féminine* 'first ascents'. For this reason perhaps the outstanding female event in the Alps in the sixties was not Daisy Voog's ascent of the Eigerwand but the two Japanese girls who in 1967 quietly climbed the north face of the Matterhorn together without fuss or fanfare.

It is in the fields of high altitude and polar climbing, which call for endurance and the ability to survive under extreme conditions rather than arm muscle and finger strength, that women are likely to excel, and one can only regret the failure to invite some of the more experienced woman climbers of the day to participate in the

Opposite: Avalanche on Mt Cook.

A V.S. lead. Sally Westmacott on the Shawangunks, USA.

expeditions which in recent years have ascended the Himalayan and Karakoram giants and converged on the South Pole. Apart from the fact that there is no reason why they should not have done as well as their male colleagues, think how much more amusing the subsequent books about the expeditions would have been. On the other hand, though it is a pity that no woman will ever be able to claim to have been the first up the world's great peaks, perhaps it is just as well. Until some really big mountain has been climbed by a purely female team it will always be difficult to refute the charge of leaning on the male. And there is still an enormous amount to be done in the Himalayas and Karakoram in the way of new routes, to say nothing, for instance, of the Kun Lun range in Sinkiang, to which some unpredictable political change may still grant the climber access.

Someone once said, 'Innocence is knowing you can and experience is knowing you can't.' In 1955, as instigator of the first woman's Himalayan expedition, my unconventional upbringing and general ignorance of the main currents of the climbing world had left me completely unaware that there was anything unusual about the idea. Having climbed happily in the Himalayas before and got on well with the Sherpas and local people, I simply wanted to go there again. The anxiety of my two companions, considerably more experienced in Scottish and guideless alpine climbing, to avoid a single mistake, not only because of its possible serious consequences but because of what their male colleagues would

Opposite: Monica Jackson at Jugalhimal Base Camp, Himalayas.

say, astonished me at first. But the deluge of warnings we received as to the likelihood of mutiny, murder and fates worse than death, to say nothing of the disasters expected to overtake us among the mountains themselves, soon convinced me that Thurber's comment, 'woman's place is in the wrong', might have been invented to fit our situation. In view of all this the enlightened attitude of the Mount Everest Foundation committee and the authorities in India and Nepal, who gave us their blessing, filled us with gratitude.

The success of this modest operation in its objective of climbing an equally modest (in Himalayan terms) mountain of 22,000 ft and exploring an unknown area, was confirmed the following year by the pioneering exploits of Eileen Healey in Kulu, where she made two or three ascents of unclimbed twenty-thousanders in the company of a few untrained Ladakhi porters and finished off by climbing Deo Tibba with them. The tragic loss in 1959 of Claude Kogan, the distinguished French mountaineer and leader of the women's Cho Oyu expedition, and her companion, was a sad setback. Claude had attempted Cho Oyu before in the company of Lambert, and as a member of a mixed party had been the first to reach the summit of the twenty-three-thousander Nun Kun. But the success of young Jo Scarr and Barbara Spark in Kulu in 1961, followed by that of the Jagdula expedition the following year, whose membership included some of Britain's best women climbers, (notably Denise Evans, Nea Morin's daughter and wife of Dr Charles Evans of Everest and Kangchenjunga fame), proved conclusively that long distance and high altitude conditions are admirably suited to the female physique. The one drawback is that a small woman may be congenitally incapable of carrying a heavy load. Claude Kogan, herself petite of frame and unable to cope with a very heavy rucksack, pointed out, 'you can't expect a donkey to carry as much as a cart-horse'. It is therefore up to the donkey to compensate by eating less or contributing to the expedition's success in some other way.

To sum up, there is potentially as much scope for the woman climber of the future as for her male counterpart, and this, if it were not for the arbitrary frontiers imposed by the cruel and absurd exigencies of politics, would still be vast. And in a sense the women are better off because so much is virgin ground for a feminine team. An all-woman ascent of the west face of the Dru or of Everest would be of great interest both scientifically because of its contribution to our knowledge of physiology and socially because of the psychological barrier to be broken down. It is really a question of getting used to the idea. Nobody is surprised when men and women meet on equal terms in horsemanship events, or that the present world champion is a woman, because the horse has been the historic means of transport and riding therefore a basic human skill. And in mountaineering our inherent ability to survive hardship is a valuable asset.

Finally, this chapter would not be complete without an acknowledgement of the support of that honourable regiment of husbands, friends, climbing colleagues, officials, and others of the opposite sex who have acted on the logical and unprejudiced assumption that female climbers, like their male equivalents, should be judged on their individual merits as people and mountaineers rather than by obsolete theories as to their fitness and capabilities. Long may they flourish and their tribe increase.

Opposite: Eileen Healey approaching Dibona.

Chapter 9

Meeting in the Hills

It augurs well for the future that such distinguished mountaineers as Lord Hunt and Eugene Gippenreiter, Master of Sport of the Soviet Union, should advocate the importance of mountains in two roles which far transcend the merely sporting

YOUTH IN THE MOUNTAINS

The Rt Hon. the Lord Hunt of Llanvair Waterdine

It is interesting to speculate to what extent the present vogue among young people for adventurous activities was stimulated by the first ascent of Everest and other exploits, such as *Kon-Tiki*, Cousteau's exploration of the ocean bed, and the various polar journeys, which have caught popular imagination. The trend certainly started earlier than 1953, in the aftermath of war, and it was to some extent inspired by adult experience of wartime mountain and commando training. Even allowing for the counter-attractions of Pop and LSD the trend among youth since 1945 has been of a much more virile kind than in the 1920s in the wake of the First World War. If delinquency of one sort and another has at the same time been a problem we must remember that a great deal of delinquency is no more than a manifestation of frustrated outlets to adventure.

The trend is not of course confined to Great Britain. There has been not inconsiderable stirring amongst the young in the United States, France and Western Germany in particular. But in Britain the problems of overcrowding and the consequent necessity to provide outlets for travel and adventure are of a much higher and more urgent degree than elsewhere. We seem to be in the van not only of the trend itself but also in the steps we are taking to channel it.

The most striking examples of this adventurous spirit are the spate of expeditions, many of them from the universities, but others also sponsored by voluntary youth organisations, local education authorities and industrial firms, which leave

About to ascend Snowdon by the Crib Goch ridge.

these shores annually for the Andes, the Himalayas, Greenland, Arctic Norway, Iceland, the Atlas or Taurus mountains or – to mention my most recent personal experience with young people – to the Pindus mountains and the Tatras in Eastern Europe. Far more expeditions with a largely youthful membership go farther afield than twenty years ago, bent on adventure mixed with just enough science to make it sound respectable to certain sources of financial support: far more, I believe, than is the case with any other country.

This is only a small part of the story of mountaineering, in its widest sense, and British youth. The number of climbing clubs in this country affiliated to the British Mountaineering Council has increased from twenty in 1944 to 141 in 1966, and the number of clubs belonging to the association of Scottish climbing clubs has almost trebled in the same period. Snow and ice climbing in Scotland has long been a regular feature of the winter and spring, providing an excellent training ground for many hundreds of young mountaineers each year. In fact, the winter standard is now so high that it has been said, with a grain of truth, that you should learn your icecraft in the Alps for Scotland rather than in Scotland for the Alps.

Organised skiing, too, has played no small part in the same movement. The National Ski Federation of Great Britain now has a membership of sixty-six clubs; with the provision of ski lifts and other facilities in the highlands Scotland has become a skiing country in her own right.

A Duke of Edinburgh's Award Scheme Gold candidate with John Hunt and Alan Blackshaw in north-east Greenland, 1960.

The Federation believes that by the provision of ski coaches and artificial slopes, skiing will become a widely popular sport throughout Britain among our young people.

So much for the van of the movement. Equally important but of much wider scope has been the growth in the popularity of less technically difficult and specialised mountain activities. The Outward Bound Trust was formed just after the war, based on wartime training experience in which I was involved myself, to administer a number of schools at which the mountains and the sea provide the basis for arduous and adventurous training of boys between sixteen and nineteen years of age. There are now six such schools in various parts of Britain, and about five thousand boys and girls pass through these schools annually. Brathay Hall, the Army Outward Bound Schools and a few other centres are comparable in that they provide four to six weeks' continuous training.

And there is a rapidly increasing number of other establishments which have also come into being to meet the demand for adventure in the mountains and the acquisition of mountaincraft, with shorter courses of weekends, weeks or fortnights. Notable among these are the Mountaineering Association, which runs training courses throughout Britain; while the Central Council of Physical Recreation and the Scottish Council respectively have permanent schools in Snowdonia and in the Cairngorms. Through these and forty to fifty other centres established in the wilder parts of Britain, staffed by qualified

Opposite: Gritstone – Almcliffe.

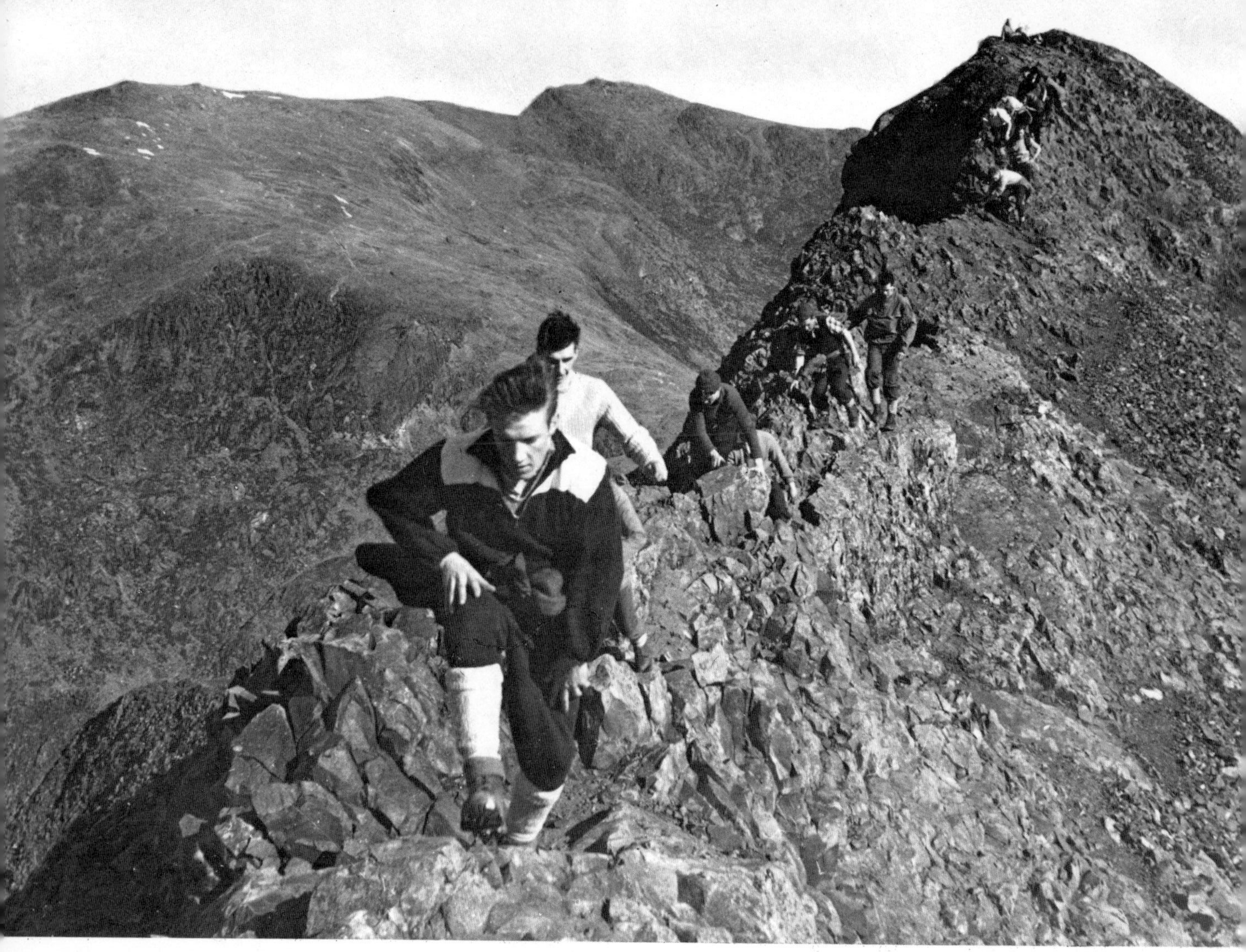

Ridge walk, an opportunity for instruction in the use of map and compass.

professional instructors and administered variously by local education authorities, youth organisations and industrial companies, thousands more young people are learning the first steps in mountaineering.

Perhaps the most significant development in recent years has been the volume of youthful journeys over the hills, 'expeditions' of two or three days' duration, as part of the extra-curricular programmes of our secondary schools, and of the outdoor activities of many youth organisations; many of these journeys form part of, or are prompted by, the Duke of Edinburgh's Award Scheme. Thousands more boys and girls go out from our cities, often during school or industrial working hours, as well as in the holidays, to learn the skills of travelling through forests, across open country, over the moors and hills, and of living out of doors.

This veritable 'explosion' of youth from our cities and plains into the hills has brought many problems in its wake. Foremost among these has been that of adequate training and preparation of inexperienced young people, to enable them to enjoy the challenge of the mountains without incurring needless risks. It was to deal with this problem that a Mountain Leadership Training Board was set up, at the initiative of the Central Council of Physical Recreation and the British Mountaineering Council, in 1963, with the co-operation of the Outward Bound Trust, the Mountaineering Association and other interested bodies. Its purpose is to administer a national certificate of competence for adults to conduct

A mixed party from a northern school taking part in a fell-walking, climbing and camping course at the Snowdonia National Recreation Centre.

young people in mountainous terrain; a similar arrangement now exists in Scotland, with an additional requirement of experience in conditions of ice and snow. The ingredients of this qualification are: an initial one-week course at a centre approved by the board, followed by a year of gaining progressive experience in the mountains, including the training of young people under qualified supervision; and a final week at an approved centre, during which the candidate's competence is assessed and instruction given in mountain rescue techniques. No certificates are granted below the age of twenty. To date 250 certificates have been earned and some 4,500 teachers, youth leaders, policemen, social workers and many others not engaged professionally in educating young people, are following the training courses at thirty approved centres in Britain. It is likely that the time will come when no headmaster will permit a member of his staff to take pupils to North Wales, the Lake District or elsewhere, unless a holder of the Mountain Leadership certificate is in charge of the group.

I can do no more in this short chapter than try to sketch the outlines of a movement of youth towards the hills which I believe to be of great importance. I am deeply persuaded that it is right to encourage youth throughout the world to find outlets for its energy, enthusiasm and enterprise, and to help them to appreciate not only the opportunities, but also the obligations and the risks.

Opposite: On the left Robin Smith, then one of Scotland's most brilliant climbers, leads the second ascent of July Crack on Great Gully Buttress, Glen Coe. His companion and the other two climbers were Soviet mountaineers, members of a goodwill visiting group.

Wilfrid Noyce and Robin Smith both lost their lives on the return visit to the Pamirs in a most unfortunate accident. But mountaineers accept the element of risk and neither, one feels, would have begrudged their lives in the cause of international goodwill and understanding – a cause they both did much to further.

MOUNTAINS MAKE PEOPLE FRIENDS *Eugene Gippenreiter* *

Friendships are most easily formed between individuals with a strong common interest. These become so much the firmer when people who share such an interest have jointly to overcome difficulties, hardships and dangers. 'Mountains make people friends'. On how many an occasion did I get convinced of the veracity of these simple words said by a Himalayan hillman, my good friend Tenzing Norkey.

On sheer rock faces covered with snow and ice each one is responsible for the security and life of his ropemate. One halves with him the last biscuit or cup of water melted from snow. It is right here, in such situations, that mutual confidence and respect are being born and friendships ripen. And I recall . . . 1958. Central Caucasus. The blizzard was roaring for three days. Tent sides of a 'British–Soviet village' were cracking in truculent gusts of wind. Tricks of fortune brought together here, at a height of about 4,000 metres on the Ushba plateau, several British and Russian mountaineers. Chris Brasher, George Band and Alan Blackshaw were evidently feeling fittest of all. In company with Anatoli Kustovski, a civil engineer from Kiev, they dug out a spacious snow cave and were having therein an international chess match in pieces made of bread crumbs. John Hunt was reading aloud in our tent a verse about a snow storm by Emerson and then a touching piece of lyric by Shelley dedicated to a skylark. . . . On leaving our mountains he said that his party regarded as their most

* Master of sport, Honorary Secretary for Foreign Relations of the Mountaineering Federation of the USSR.

important achievement the friendships made with a large number of Soviet mountaineers and that they believed these contacts between mountain lovers were of great value and a contribution to a better understanding between our countries.

. . . 1960. North Wales. The Cirp Las summit was not far when I saw a piece of chocolate on a cliff ledge. Hunt (he was leading) turned and with a warm friendly smile repeated the words from a film about the traverse of formidable Ushba called 'If Mountains Could Speak' . . ., words 'uttered' by Ushba herself: 'Can't understand you people. Do you always look after each other or only when in difficulty? This question makes me uneasy each time I see people on these rocks'. In this film shown at the Alpine Club, our mountaineers did the same, leaving small bits of chocolate on snow for those who were following them. . . . Sports school at Plas-y-Brenin. Having looked round it, we accepted with pleasure an invitation to go boating in a canoe on a local lake. The outcome was unexpectedly quick: hardly had we covered several dozen metres from the bank when our canoe turned over and a moment later, surely through the sense of solidarity, M. Kherghiani flew into the water from another boat right in the middle of the lake. Having hardly managed to scramble out to the bank (he nearly went to the bottom in clothes and heavy mountain boots) and with chattering teeth after an icy-cold bath, my boat companion Hunt muttered that it was indeed just another ordeal to experience for the sake of promoting British–Soviet co-operation.

. . . 1962. Pamir. 'Union Jack' and 'Sickle and Hammer' flutter side by side above base camp, pitched in the forest near the tongue of the Garmo Glacier. There comes our first evening in the mountains. We decide to share tents on 'mixed ropes' principle. One can hear some puffing, exclamations of surprise, then a burst of laughter from one of the tents. It turns out that Robin Smith and Anatoli Ovchinnikov have been trying in vain to inflate an air mattress until they discovered that an English word, 'hole' and a Russian one 'dyra', meant one and the same thing. During the expedition, among other peaks, we made a pioneer ascent of a 'six thousander' and gave it the name of 'Concord Peak'. Having sent us a colour picture of this beautiful summit our British friends wrote that Concord Peak was a solid monument to our common belief in the ideals shared by us and to our hopes that other people would also show similar examples of true comradeship and friendship. In his interview to a *Daily Mail* correspondent, John Hunt, leader of the first British–Soviet high-altitude expedition, stressed that the joint adventure had helped us to become true friends who understood and respected the views of each other.

Climbing being over, everyone returns to his everyday business. However, ties of friendship established in the hills do not weaken. 'Comrade Ralph' sends to his ropemate 'Mister Joseph' (for such is the way R. Jones, an Englishman, and J. Khahiani, a hillman from Suanetia, call each other) a big photo in memory of their joint ascent and advises him that his young son's addiction to pranks undoubtedly deserves the epithet 'terrible' to his Russian name 'Ivan'. A Scotchman Graham Nicol writes to his teammate Vladimir Malakhov, a Russian engineer, that he is still unmarried and intends to come to Moscow for a Russian bride. It is with courage that Mrs M. C. B. Smith met the news about the tragic death of her only son Robin in the Pamirs. She wrote to his friends in Moscow that she was not rich and had only a small house but there

Opposite: North Ridge, Alpamayo.
Overleaf: Moulin.

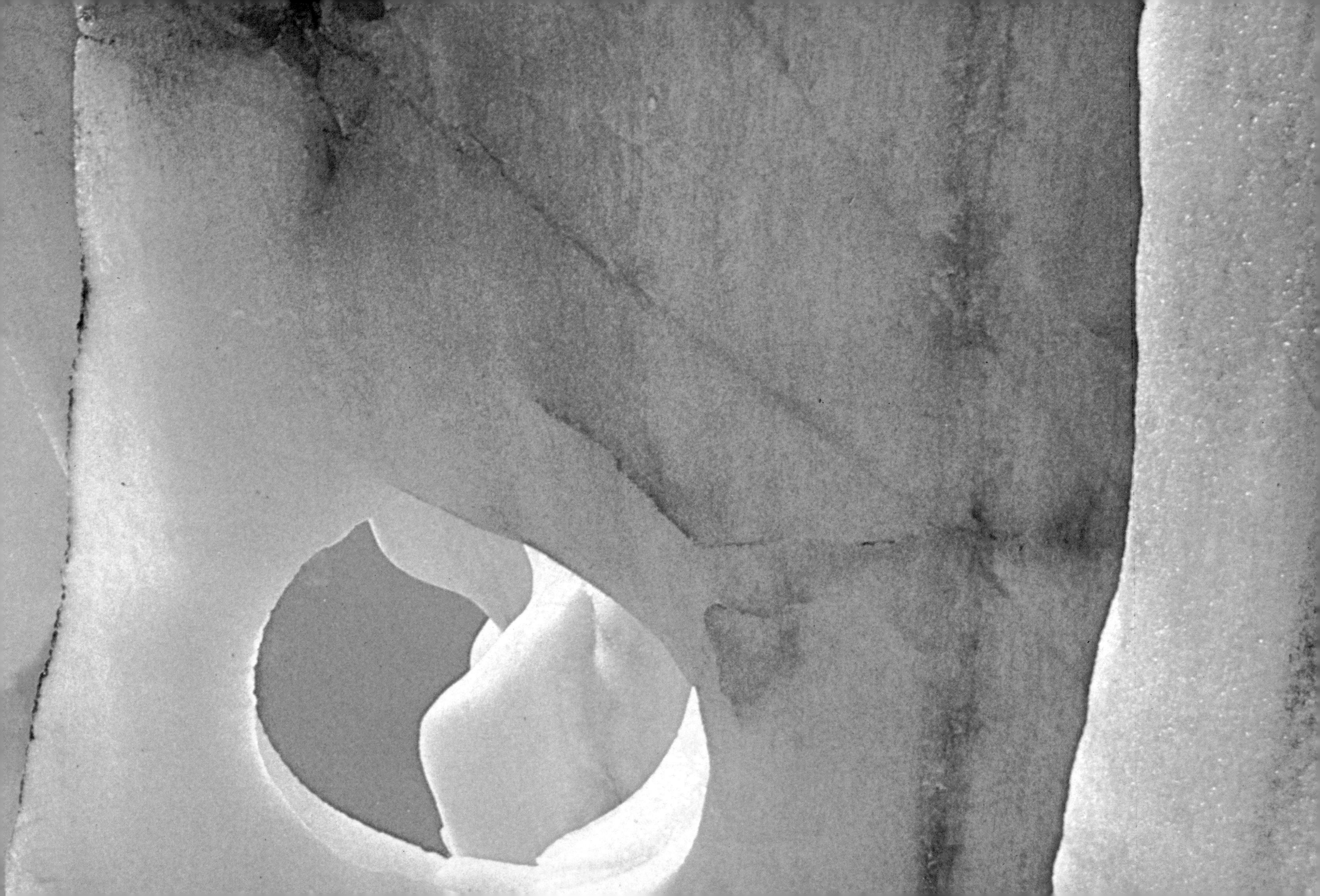

would always be a bed for one or two Soviet climbers in her house.

Climbers of the world make one team united by a strong rope of international friendship. Close contacts between mountain lovers are of great value, for they improve mutual understanding among countries and contribute to a noble mission of creating mutual confidence and goodwill among nations. Sports brotherhood created and cemented during difficult ascents facilitates understanding between people and thus it is a pledge of peace.

In summer 1967 an international Alpiniad to Lenin peak dedicated to the fiftieth anniversary of the Soviet State, was carried out in the Pamirs. 31 climbers from nine countries of Europe reached the top (7,134 metres). Before the start of this undertaking Italian participants underlined that they approached mountaineering as a sport of individuals, not as a collective venture. On completion of the ascent of Lenin Peak, the leader of the Italian party, Emilio Frisia, stated that only through the close-knit nature of the expedition and comradely mutual aid could they have reached the summit of this 'seven thousander'. According to Stanislaw Biel, leader of the Polish team, such a mass assault could have been carried out successfully by all the participants owing to a strong 'feeling of elbow' and cordial friendship. The Austrian alpinists climbed Lenin Peak by its east face. Eric Vanis, leader of their party, stated they had succeeded in doing it thanks to an atmosphere of friendship and mutual aid among members of the joint enterprise. 'When someone felt unwell', he continued, 'doctors from all other delegations were in a hurry to help him'.

'I wish that it might be possible to multiply the contacts between ordinary folk like ourselves . . . Therein lies the best hope of realising a true brotherhood of man.' In such words, full of hopes for peace in the world, Lord Hunt concludes *The Red Snows*, a book published in London soon after the trip to the Caucasus.

Opposite: Women's party in the Himalayas.

Chapter 10

Mountains and the Mind of Man

Has the advent of artificial climbing and the conquest of a hundred routes not so long ago thought to be impossible, together with recent scientific advances of immediate benefit to the mountaineer, radically changed man's attitude to mountains? Is there, perhaps, a new philosophy and a new mysticism? Four very different authorities ponder these questions, each in his own way

MOUNTAIN MYSTICISM *Arnold Lunn*

Mountaineering is perhaps the only sport in which some of its devotees have attempted to find a substitute for religion, a development which was perhaps influenced by the fact that the foundation of the Alpine Club coincided with a particularly confident attack on Christianity. It is an interesting coincidence that *The Origin of Species* and *Peaks, Passes, and Glaciers* should both have been published in 1859. Leslie Stephen, who had been an Anglican priest before he wrote *An Agnostic's Apology*, was not the only mountaineer in whom mountains evoked something faintly reminiscent of that sense of worship which had been evoked by the religion in which they had ceased to believe. 'If I were to invent a new idolatry', he wrote, 'I should prostrate myself not before beast or ocean or sun, but before one of those mighty masses to which, in spite of all reason, it is impossible not to attribute some shadowy personality. Their voice is mystic and has found discordant interpreters; but to me at least it speaks in tones at once more tender and more awe-inspiring than that of any mortal teacher.'

Under the influence of Leslie Stephen I rejected Christianity while still at school and explored the possibilities of materialism. I am essentially a rationalist whose beliefs have been formed by examining the available evidence, and only once in my life have I felt that some aspect of ultimate truth had been revealed to me. I was nineteen at the time, an agnostic if not an atheist by belief. I was resting after a climb on an alpine pass after a sunset hour of supreme beauty. And

Opposite: In Karwendel.

suddenly I knew beyond immediate need of proof that a beauty which was not of this world was revealed in the visible loveliness of the mountains. This experience was of value not as evidence of truth but as a stimulus to research, and in due course I discovered that no *purely* materialistic theory of evolution, as for instance natural selection or the survival of the fittest, offers the slightest clue to the origin of our sense of beauty, but I always realised the limitations of what may be called mountain mysticisms. Charles Meade, the famous Himalayan explorer, wisely insists that 'Whatever importance nature-mysticism may have in its relation to religious mysticism is due to its potentially preparatory character', and he might have quoted in support of this sound observation Philo's 'All Nature is the language in which God expresses his thoughts but the thoughts are more important than the language.' In a brilliant paper read before the Alpine club the late Michael Roberts reminded us that 'mountains may be symbols or images of some other reality, but the worship of images as if they were something more than images is a form of superstition', or, rather, a form of idolatry in the strict sense of the term. And all those who explicitly profess to believe in 'the religion of the mountains' must indeed be prepared to defend themselves against the accusation of mountain idolatry. Frank Smythe was the most influential and the most widely read of those who have attempted to construct an alpine theology without mentioning Theos and who have been explicit in writing about 'the religion of the mountains'. His variety of mountain mysticism appealed to many who could not accept any form of institutional religion. He was one of the outstanding mountaineers of his generation, with a highly personal gift for describing mountain adventure. There was genuine mysticism in his response to mountain beauty, and there were many moving passages in his books in which he was content to recall without attempting to explain the happiness which he had found in the hills. He resolutely refused to read anything about religion or mysticism because, so he told me, he wanted to be sure that his interpretation of mountain mysticism was his own and not confused by anything which he might have read by others. He never considered the possibility that such reading might have clarified rather than confused his mountain philosophy; might, for instance, have helped him to distinguish between the worship of mountains which is ridiculous and the worship inspired by mountains which is anything but ridiculous, and to eliminate from his admirable mountaineering books such meaningless utterances as 'those who are impelled towards the hills seek something finer than the man-made dogmas now crushing and distorting the spiritual teaching of the universe'. 'The religion of the mountains', he tells us, 'is not one of cant or ritual', but whereas cant is always objectionable, ritual is often desirable. After describing a dangerous descent in a thunderstorm

Opposite: Riessersee.
Overleaf: 'Mountains may be symbols or images of some other reality'.

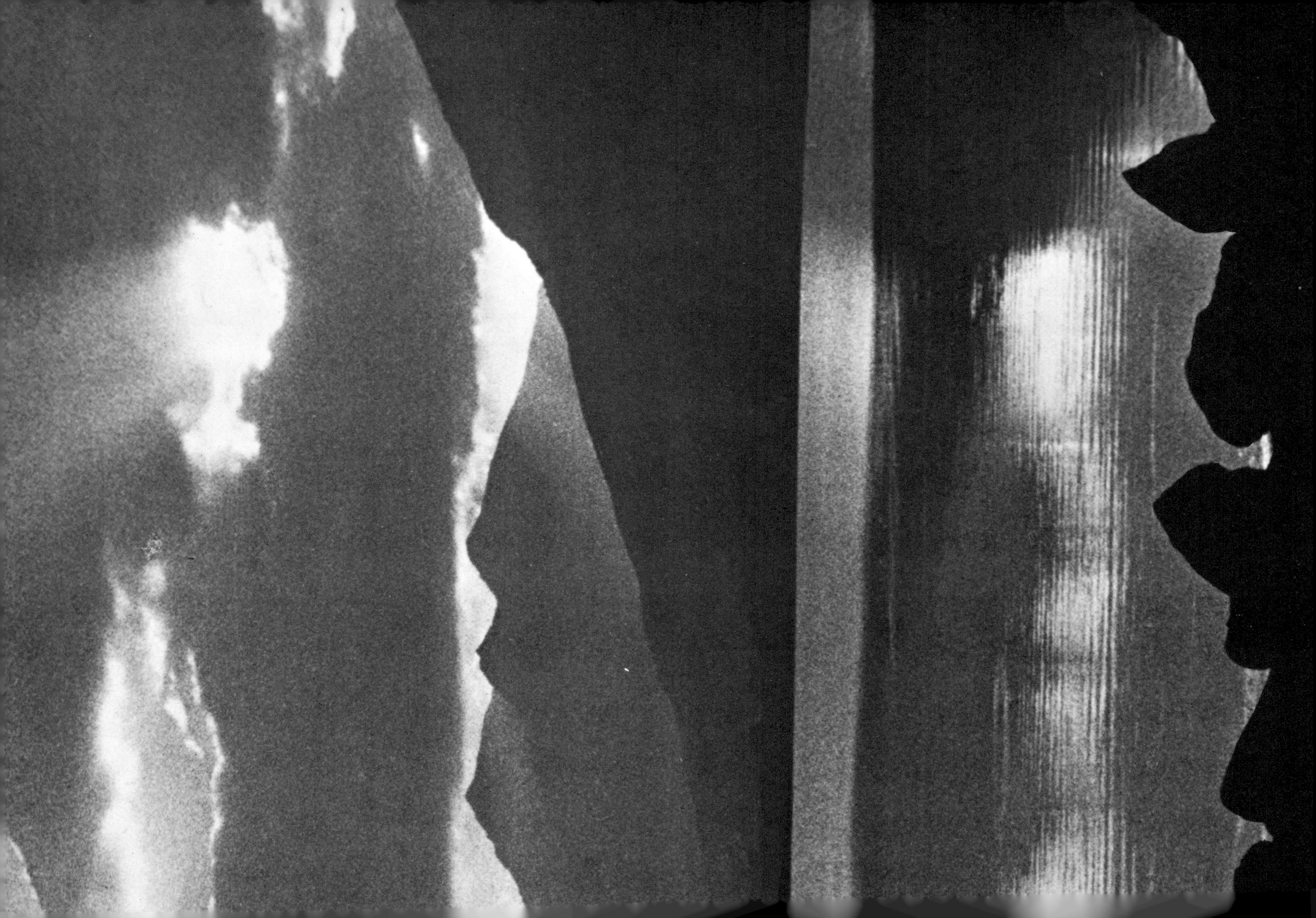

Smythe writes: 'There, with nothing but easy ground separating us from the hut, we shook hands not without feeling, for it had been a close thing.' In the ritual of this handshake their corporate gratitude for escape from a common peril was appropriately expressed. Though Smythe's attempt to construct a religion out of mountaineering was unconvincing, his undoubted distinction as a mountain writer owed a great deal to his passionate conviction that no purely physical explanation could account for the adoration evoked in him by the beauty of the mountains.

Geoffrey Winthrop Young's *On High Hills* was perhaps the most brilliant book of mountain adventure written in this century, and he certainly had no rivals as a mountain poet. I must, however, admit that the exposition of his mountain philosophy in the concluding pages of *On High Hills* conveyed no clear meaning to me. I could find nothing in those pages with which I could either agree or disagree. I suspect that he was too diffident to express in prose the mountain mysticism which is the inspiration of the finest poems in *Wind and Hill*. Young was an agnostic so far as his own response to mountain beauty was concerned. Why mountains moved him as they did he did not *know*, but he could express in poetry what he *felt*. There were at least some moods in which he felt that something of him would survive in the mountains

> The best of us, the soul we never lost
> Shall join that host upon the cloud-girt stair.
> Selfless, a part of all we loved the most
> Friends of the Mountains, you will find us there.

And perhaps the mountain mysticism, which he would never have explicitly avowed in prose, is the inspiration of his poem *On the Mountain*. Was he sometimes conscious among the mountains of an unseen companion, or was there absolutely nothing in his own experience, not even a passing fancy, which found expression in these lines?

> I never see him, but his tread
> Sounds just before my own;
> One thought designs the task of day,
> One effort wins the onward way
> Dividing, yet alone;
> Swayed by one resolute consent
> Of sympathy unsaid.

Explicit attempts to interpret the mystical element in our love of mountains are rare in mountain literature, and often find expression only in a few lines of a long chapter, as for instance in this sentence in a paper which F. W. Bourdillon contributed to Vol. xxiv of the *Alpine Journal*:

> We have all of us had our 'moments', either on the mountains, or perhaps in some distant view of them, when life and joy have assumed new meanings, and the world's horizons suddenly broken down and shown us realms of dream beyond and yet beyond.

or R. L. G. Irving's confession in Vol. xxv of the *Alpine Journal* that for the mountaineer 'with each succeeding year grows an abiding conviction in the dependence of himself and his surroundings on the benevolence of some unseen power'.

Infinitely the most important of all religious or philosophical distinctions is the difference between those who believe that ultimate reality is spiritual and those who believe that ultimate reality is material, and for this if for no other reason it seems to me worth while to record the modest contribution which mountaineers and mountain lovers have made to a spiritual interpretation of the universe.

Entrance to Rongbuk valley, Tibet: a picture taken in 1924 by N. E. Odell. From the right: George Mallory, Bentley Beetham, Andrew Irvine.

PARTING OF THE WAYS? *Anthony Rawlinson*

Other controversies about mountaineering innovations – guideless climbing, crampons, skiing, oxygen, rubber shoes – have died in time. Will the controversy about artificial climbing go the same way, or are they right who see in it a lasting schism in the mountaineering world? On some new climbs in recent years, for example the big Yosemite routes in the United States and in the Alps on the west face of the Dru and the direct route up the Eigerwand, pitons and slings and all the paraphernalia of artificial techniques have been used continuously for many hundreds of feet. Do such climbs indicate a parting of the ways between 'mountaineers' and 'engineers'?

It is not necessary to share the disapproval generally implied in the term 'engineers' to find some grounds for differentiation. New types of piton, so that almost any crack in the rock can be used, drill and expansion bolts when cracks are lacking, light hammocks so that a rock ledge is no longer necessary even to pass the night – by these and other devices almost any rock face reasonably free from objective dangers of loose or falling rock must now be regarded as climbable, given time. (If artificial techniques are less extensively applied to ice, it is only because the problems of objective danger are usually greater there.) With modern food and bivouac equipment, ascents can be spread over many days, or even weeks. Time and logistics replace technical difficulty at the heart of the climbing problem. This is certainly a new kind of climbing.

These evident changes mask a change in the nature of climbing itself. In 'conventional' climbing, the physical configuration of the mountain is a fixed element. The climber climbs by making the movements of his body a variable. His agility and skill is to adapt his body to the shape of the mountain. There is a limit to his capacity to adapt. When the shape of the mountain lies beyond that limit, he cannot climb it. In artificial climbing the mountain is no longer a fixed element; it too becomes a variable. The climber's agility, his capacity to adapt, is still limited, but he uses his pitons to adapt the mountain so as to bring it within his own limitations. Since in principle there need be no limit to this process, anything becomes climbable – which is not to say that artificial techniques are easy, for they are not.

Whether these subtleties are of practical importance is perhaps debatable. More often the subject of comment by critics of artificial climbing are ways in which the attitude of the young climbers who practise it differ from their own. It is sometimes charged, for example, that they lack the traditional aesthetic appreciation of mountains. Although there are other and more important factors involved here, it is probably true that with its slow rate of progress and need for unremitting concentration on the technicalities, artificial climbing presents more restricted opportunities for aesthetic experience than the relatively rapid changes of scene and atmosphere in conventional climbing.

In these and other ways it is easy to point to new features which artificial climbing has introduced into mountaineering. Yet one may doubt whether they are really as divisive as controversialists represent.

If there is such a schism as suggested, it is surprisingly difficult to define just where it lies. Almost all the leading exponents of artificial climbing whose activities provoke the controversy also do a great deal of conventional mountaineering, often of the highest class. Meanwhile, whatever may have been true in the past, few parties today visit major, or even minor, mountains without carrying pitons and using them from time to time. So the controversy, in its current form, concerns degree rather than principle. Distinctions of degree seldom last long.

Perhaps the heart of the matter lies in the changes in attitudes already mentioned. Attitudes do change from one generation to another. There is nothing new or surprising in this. Nor need it be assumed that the change is necessarily for the worse. The outlook of the present generation of climbers is not in all respects the same as that of their elders, nor is the attitude to artificial climbing by any means the only factor in this. But these differences between generations are probably less than either party thinks. They are exaggerated as much by the young as by the old. Both overlook how much they have in common: the same mountains, the same adventure in climbing them, the same fascination in overcoming the challenge of difficulty, the same search for novelty which is inherent in all the best adventure. If the moderns use artificial methods, it is chiefly because their elders have left so little that is new to do by other means. It is unbecoming on the part of the elders to grudge to their successors the pleasures of novelty which they themselves enjoyed. Rather, older mountaineers should seek to share in the excitement of the new horizons which artificial climbing is opening. There may be an occasional abortive by-way; but in the main artificial climbing is not a departure from the high road of mountaineering history: it is the gateway to its continuation and the future.

Opposite: Dougal Haston on the Old Man of Hoy.

CLIMBERS *James Morris*

There is no denying that in externals climbers have changed. Innocents who go to mountaineering inns anticipating a fragrance of dons, pipe tobacco and leather map-cases, may expect to be disillusioned, as they sidle their way through the babel of rude language, the blodges of large pink thighs, the clutter of nylon ropes, bottles and miscellaneous spiky things that are the prerequisites of modern alpinism. It is a long time, I think, since a classicist read his *Religio Medici* over the Gentleman's Relish, before setting off with his friend, the incumbent of Brambletree Magna, on another demanding ascent.

But in deeper essentials the sport is very resilient – by which I mean that it remains to the outsider perfectly inexplicable, and indeed rather ludicrous. In the century odd since men started to climb for pleasure, nobody has really succeeded in explaining what the pleasure is, and climbers have remained from that day to this testily on the defensive. Like any other comical minority they take their foibles seriously, seeking to prove that if a pastime cannot logically be fun, then it must have meaning – like the man Kinglake quoted in *Eothen*, who habitually retreated when a joke fell flat to the assertion that anyway it was *true*.

So the fact that it is all perfectly useless has given mountaineering its nimbus of mysticism – enshrined once and for all in Mallory's ultimate bathos, 'because it's there'. Climbing is not, like tennis or water-skiing, an absolute occupation. You absolutely must hit a ball with a racket to play tennis, just as there is no substitute in kind for a pair of water-skis: but in most instances you

Two 'piton modernists' – Royal Robbins and Tom Frost.

can reach the summit of a mountain, or the top of a rock face, by some easier means than climbing. Mountaineers are accordingly obsessed by the reason why. They anticipate the question every time, with skimble-skamble stuff (for there is a good deal of Welshness to their attitudes) about challenge, solitude and vision.

I don't know how the piton modernists explain their sport, which seems to consist of choosing the hardest possible place to climb, and then making it artificially easier: for to tell you the truth, fighting shy as I do of too many beards and bulging muscles, I have never summoned up the nerve to ask – expecting to be rebuffed with some modernist oath, or throatily laughed at. But I have a very strong feeling that the rationale, such as it is, has not much progressed, and that the vicar of Brambletree Magna would soon feel himself at home if deposited among the spilt beer and potato crisps of his successors. A fence separates climbers from the rest of the world, and there on the other side of it, old or young, earthy or urbane, down the decades they happily exchange the jargon of their beloved and arcane cult.

MOUNTAINS AND THE MIND OF MAN *Charles Houston*

It's not difficult to imagine what Hannibal thought of the mountains as he led his elephants across a snowy pass to attack Rome: they shielded his campaign, permitting surprise, but they were also dangerous, difficult and to be avoided when possible . . . The ancient Greeks shunned the mountains lest they offend the gods who lived among the clouds; Asiatics thought the mountains holy and worshipped the eternal snows. . . . Alpine valley dwellers climbed only to hunt for game or gems; they thought the mountains inhabited by fire-breathing dragons and other horrors. . . . Climbing for sport is something rather recent.

Conrad Gessner in 1555 was the first to write with admiration of the mountains as a source of pleasure. In 1786 Mont Blanc was climbed – partly because it was the highest point in Europe, partly for fame and gain – but also for sport. However, not for almost another century did climbing become popular. The golden age of alpine climbing ran from 1850 to 1870; in that short period most of the summits were reached by sportsmen – mainly British – romping over what Sir Leslie Stephen called 'the playground of Europe'. A little later the Andes and Rockies were explored and climbed and more recently the enormous wilds of the Himalayas. Will tomorrow be the age of mountaineering on the moon or other distant ranges? Must man always push against the limits of the possible?

The game of climbing has much to commend it: there is the excitement of danger, all levels of challenge to skill, great beauty and wildness, and

Sledge party, Victoria land.

Overleaf: The Jungfrau is a young lady of many different moods: in summer, high above the valley haze, she can be golden and infinitely remote. In the cold sharp air of winter every detail of her face stands out with vivid clarity. She is never less than beautiful and if the truth were known this view of her from Interlaken must many times have drawn men away from their homes and families to search among the high hills for they knew not quite what.

above all in these congested times – there is space. It may be played solo for greater risk and thrill, or as a team where inter-dependence breeds deep friendship. It can be contemplative, philosophic, or intensely chauvinistic and competitive. The ardent mountaineer may disguise his passion as science – and many felt compelled to do so in the last century – or he may be unabashedly a mountain buff. Psychiatrists think the climber is sublimating forbidden phallic or oedipal urges.

Mummery described a mountain's changing reputation: 'an inaccessible peak, the most difficult ascent in the Alps, an easy day for a lady', a progression due to performance by a new generation incredible to its forebears. Anything can be climbed by the determined, strong, and well-equipped party: today's acrobat won't begin without a weight of nails and bolts and stirrups, though use of such hardware might bar him for life from the best alpine clubs fifty years ago. With today's tools even the ultimate overhang of ice may be climbed: does this mean that the challenge is gone? He who tackles the ultimate climbs will be watched by plane and television; he may later write, speak, or appear around the world for money. Small wonder there is national competition for the highest or most dangerous peaks.

But there are still many who climb quietly for joy, peace, release of tension, for the pleasures of fitness and to bask in beauty. Others must test limits of nerve, strength and skill in a way denied to the earthbound. Man seems unique among animals in such deliberate self-testing. Each generation tries, and often achieves, what its parents found impossible. Perhaps man must always reach beyond his grasp and by so reaching, grow, perhaps even to a day when he is at peace with others.

Let climbing be such a test, a challenge, a danger, and a gauge of skill for those who wish. But let us keep the mountains clean and above petty national and individual competition. Mountains are never 'conquered': perhaps for a few moments in the great space of time a puny man may stand on a mountain top without being beaten by storm, but men don't conquer mountains any more than mountains conquer men. As swaggering boastful men stand briefly on those summits, let them not lose their perspective, nor forget by what tolerance they are there.

Notes on Contributors

RENNIE BERE
For five years Director and Chief Warden, Uganda National Parks; publications include mountaineering and wild life works; possesses an exhaustive knowledge of the Ruwenzori.

T. S. BLAKENEY
Former tea planter, South India. Assistant Secretary of the Alpine Club, 1948–58; Secretary of the Mount Everest Foundation since 1958. Author of a long series of erudite and scholarly papers on the history, personalities and minutiae of the sport.

CHRISTIAN BONINGTON
Mountaineer, photographer and author/journalist. Made the first British ascent of the Eigerwand, first ascents of Annapurna II, Nuptse and Central Tower, Cordillera Paine together with a number of 'very severe' firsts on rock.

F. R. BROOKE
Naval Officer (retired). Member of the British North Greenland Expedition 1952–4; of the Trans-Antarctic Expedition (Hillary's party) 1957–8; and of the Rakaposki Expedition.

IAN CLOUGH
Formerly RAF Mountain Rescue now a professional climbing instructor in Glen Coe; made the first British ascent of the Eigerwand (with Bonington); leader of the 1967–8 Joint British Patagonian Expedition (which made the first ascent of the Fortress).

GÜNTER AND NORMAN DYHRENFURTH
G. O. Dyhrenfurth is a distinguished Swiss geographer and geologist; a leading authority on the Himalayas he was leader of the Kangchenjunga (1930) and Karakoram (1934) expeditions. His son, Norman, an American national, is a motion picture producer and explorer: leader of the highly successful 1963 American Everest Expedition and a member of four other Himalayan parties including the 1952 Swiss Everest Expedition.

COLIN FRASER
An agricultural expert with a fluent command of several European languages deeply interested in skiing and mountaineering. His publications include *The Avalanche Enigma* – a masterly study of a perennial mountain hazard.

EUGENE GIPPENREITER
A first class mountaineer and Master of Sport of the Soviet Union. He is at present Honorary Secretary for Foreign Relations of the Mountaineering Federation of the USSR.

A. H. GRIFFIN
Author and broadcaster and a leading authority on the history, customs and mountains of his home country – the Lakeland. He is a rock climber and skier.

J. M. HARTOG
Scientist, currently engaged upon nuclear research; his greatest mountain feat was the first ascent of the formidable Muztagh Tower.

CHARLES HOUSTON
A distinguished American medical scientist and mountaineer: member of several important expeditions including Mt Foraker (1934), Nanda Devi (1936), K2 (1938 and 1953) and Everest Reconnaissance (1950).

THE RT HON. THE LORD HUNT OF LLANVAIR WATERDINE
Professional soldier and mountaineer who led the successful assault on Everest in 1953 he is perhaps best known for his outstanding work in the field of youth welfare. As Director for ten years of the Duke of Edinburgh's Award Scheme, and in a dozen advisory capacities, he has done much towards both pointing the need, and providing the means, to guide the young towards a true spirit of adventure. He is also a strong protagonist of the value of international mountaineering.

MONICA JACKSON
Married, mother of two; has climbed extensively in the Alps, Himalayas, the Atlas, Great Britain and Turkish Kurdistan – where she took part in the first *cordée féminine* ascent of Rezko Tepe.

JOHN LONGLAND
Market manager, son of 'Everester' Jack Longland; alpinist, member of 1957 Pumisillo Expedition.

SIR ARNOLD LUNN
In his youth (before a severe accident put an end to his climbing) a competent mountaineer with a number of first ascents on skis to his credit. Author of over fifty philosophical, mountaineering and skiing works, and editor of six numbers of the Alpine Ski Club Annual followed by forty-eight numbers of its successor, the British Ski Year Book. He played a leading role in the development of international competitive skiing.

C. DOUGLAS MILNER
In professional life, a bank manager: author of books and articles on mountaineering subjects and a noted mountain photographer.

TERRIS MOORE
An Honorary Professor, and former President, of the University of Alaska distinguished both as mountaineer and aviator. His first ascents include Sangay (1929), Mt Bona (1930), Mt Fairweather (1931), Minya Konka (1932) and Mt Sanford (1938). In the 1950s he pioneered glacier landing techniques with a Piper Super Cub giving invaluable support to climbing parties on Mt McKinley and landing on the summits of Mts Wrengell and Sanford.

JAMES MORRIS
Eminent author and journalist whose first acquaintance with mountaineers was when he was appointed Times Special Correspondent to the 1953 Everest Expedition. 'Since then,' he later wrote, 'I have extended my range of technical experience to several of the more severe ascents in the Malvern Hills'.

W. H. MURRAY
Author and journalist and notable Scottish climber who was a member of the 1951 Reconnaissance Expedition to Everest and of other Himalayan parties.

N. E. ODELL
A distinguished geologist; member of the 1924 and 1938 Everest expeditions; made the first

ascent of Nanda Devi in 1936 and has climbed extensively in the Alps, Canada and New Zealand.

T. W. PATEY

A magnificent all-round mountaineer he made the first ascent of the Muztagh Tower in 1956 and of Rakaposhi in 1958. He practices as a doctor in Ullapool and has played a notable part in recent developments in Scottish winter climbing techniques including a number of winter 'firsts'. Writes, sings and broadcasts songs of climbers and climbing.

E. C. PYATT

Civil servant and author; an authority on the history of climbing in Great Britain whose favourite district is North Wales.

ANTHONY RAWLINSON

A treasury official who is a good enough mountaineer to have been a 'reserve' for Everest in 1953. Honorary Secretary of the Alpine Club 1963–6: he possesses a wide knowledge of the contemporary mountain scene.

ROYAL ROBBINS

Businessman, former professional ski and climbing instructor. He is an outstanding rock technician who played an important part in the development of American climbing 'hardware', particularly the range of rock pitons and sky-hooks.

ANDRÉ ROCH

Skier, mountaineer, explorer, writer and photographer now a senior member of the staff of the Swiss Federal Avalanche Research Station, Davos.

GEORGE R. SAINSBURY

A past chairman of the Mountain Rescue Council and one of the founders of the Mountain Rescue Association of America; member of the Board of Councillors of The American Alpine Club.

E. E. SHIPTON

One of the greatest mountaineer-explorers of all time. Leader of two Everest reconnaissance parties, five expeditions to the mountains of East and Central Africa, the Karakoram 1939 Expedition, the 1952 British Himalayan Expedition and of six expeditions to Patagonia; member of three Everest and several other Himalayan expeditions including the party that conquered Kamet in 1931. Author of a number of notable mountain and travel works.

H. W. TILMAN

Soldier, Kenya farmer, mountaineer, traveller, author and deep water sailor; highlights of a life which he continues to pack with adventure include service with the Albanian Partisans, leadership of the 1938 Everest Expedition, travel and mountain conquests in Sinkiang, Nepal, Greenland, Central Africa and Patagonia and many notable voyages in his cutter *Mischief* across some of the most hostile seas in the world.

MICHAEL WARD

A consultant surgeon; has climbed and skied in Europe, North America and the Himalayas. Member of the 1951 and 1953 Everest Expeditions, first ascent of Amadablam and led the ascent on Makalu after Edmund Hillary's illness. Carried out high altitude research in 1960–1, spending the winter at 19,000 ft, and in 1964 and 1965 led geographical exploration and medical research parties in North Bhutan.

Glossary

ABSEIL: descent with the aid of a doubled rope placed round a convenient rock bollard or through a sling which itself may be attached to a piton or combination of pitons. The sling must be left but the rope can be pulled down after the last man.

A.C.: The Alpine Club.

ALP: in summer a mountain pasture normally found above the zone of glacial over-deepening of mountain valleys.

ANORAK: a ski or climbing jacket with hood.

ARÊTE: a narrow snow or rock ridge.

ARTIFICIAL CLIMBING: climbing with the assistance of bolts, skyhooks pitons and wedges both for protection and, in many situations, for direct support.

AVALANCHE: a cascade of snow, ice or rocks (or a combination of these) down a mountain side.

BELAY: a projection to which the climber can secure himself. Where natural belays are absent pitons can be used.

BERGSCHRUND: the crevasse, often a large one, which separates the moving ice of a glacier from the static ice or rock face above.

BINDINGS: the devices which attach the skis to the boots. Modern bindings (including those used by ski mountaineers) open under strong forward or rotational forces and are commonly known as 'safety' or 'release' bindings.

BIVOUAC: a night spent in the open, either by error of judgement or by deliberate intent, during the course of a climb.

BOLLARD (ICE): a large mushroom-like projection of ice hewn out of an ice slope round which a belay rope can be passed, nowadays rendered obsolete by ice-pitons.

BOSSE (*French*): a dome of snow, rock or ice.

BRÈCHE (*French*): a gap in a ridge too small to be called a Col.

CAGOULE (*French*): a knee-length smock with a hood.

CHIMNEY: a vertical or near vertical crack big enough to allow the climber to enter.

Glossary

CHOCKSTONE: a wedged stone.

COL: a depression on a mountain ridge.

CORNICE: overhanging snow or ice along a ridge or in area of abrupt change of slope, caused by the wind.

COULOIR: a gulley.

CRAMPONS: set of metal spikes strapped to the boots, used by mountaineers to procure a foothold on ice or hard snow.

CREVASSE: a fissure in a glacier most frequently found at a point of change of slope or direction; often very deep; most crevasses are plugged with snow in winter.

CWM: a scoop or enclosed valley high on the slopes of a mountain probably caused by the action of ice in a period of (geologically) recent glaciation. In the United Kingdom Cwms – which are also known as Corries – frequently hold a small tarn or lochan.

DRY GLACIER: a glacier that bears no snow on the surface of the ice.

EDGING: forcing the edges of the skis into the slope by pressing the knees forward and inward; an essential manoeuvre for the ski mountaineer who frequently must traverse steep exposed slopes of hard snow.

EXPANSION BOLT: an item of artificial climbing equipment borrowed from the builder: requires a hole to be drilled in the rock (itself probably no mean effort) before it can be used.

FACE: the precipitous side of a mountain, named for the direction in which it faces (the North Face of the Eiger faces north etc.).

FIRN SNOW: Spring snow resembling granulated sugar, formed by freeze and thaw, common in high snow mountains in spring and summer.

FREE CLIMBING: in its purest form the climbing of a pitch by a leader with no support or protection other than the support and protection afforded to him by his second. The expression, however, is coming increasingly to mean the climbing of a pitch without artificial aids for support – the leader being permitted to leave a series of pitons etc. behind him for protection.

GENDARME: a rock tooth or tower on a ridge.

GIPFEL (*German*): a summit.

GLACIER: a flowing mass of ice; the rate of movement – which is governed by the gradient and the incidence of precipitation – varies between a few centimetres and several hundred metres a year.

GLISSADE: sliding down a steep slope using the boots as though they are skis; the ice-axe is an aid in controlling speed and direction.

GRAT (*German*): ridge.

ICE-AXE: the classical design consists of ash shaft with steel head, the latter bearing a 'pick' and an 'adze'. There are now all-metal ice-axes on the market adapted for use with artificial aids.

ICE-FALL: a highly crevassed, broken area of a glacier commencing at a point where there is a sharp increase in the slope of the underlying terrain; the termination of a hanging glacier (see Sérac).

JOCH (*German*): a pass or neck joining two higher portions of a mountain chain.

JUG HANDLE: a fine, 'thank God' handhold.

JUMAR CLIP: a metal clip which can be slid up the rope but which holds firmly when the climber's weight comes onto it. Used, in place of the old 'prussic slings', to climb a rope.

KARABINER: metal clip-ring the snap-link sometimes secured, for greater safety, with a screw collar.

LEAD THROUGH: two climbers leading alternate pitches.

MONSOON: a wind which blows in India and South East Asia reversing its direction in winter and summer, blowing south-westerly in the latter season.

MORAINE: a terminal moraine consists of rock debris deposited by a glacier at its tongue; a lateral moraine flanks a glacier and is formed by material falling from adjacent cliffs. If two glaciers converge the two inner lateral moraines will combine to form a medial moraine.

MUNRO: a Scottish mountain over 3,000 ft in height.

NÉVÉ (*French*): consolidated Firn snow.

PITCH: a stretch of difficult rock, snow or ice between places where the second can halt and support his leader.

PITON: a metal spike with a ring or hole at one end. Pitons are of a great variety of sizes and shapes and are driven into cracks in the rock or screwed or driven into ice with the object of providing direct support for the climber (in which case étriers can be clipped into a karabiner, which itself has been affixed to the piton) or of supplying a belaying point for the leader or other member of the party. Pitons can also be left at intervals on a difficult pitch so as to give the leader nearer protection than can be afforded him by his second.

PORTERS: the mountaineers' professional assistants whose duty it is to carry equipment and stores.

POWDER SNOW: low temperature snow, light and loose, eminently attractive to the skier but a bane to the mountaineer.

RUN OUT: in free climbing the length of rope between the leader and his second.

SANGAR: a windbreak in the form of a low wall of rock or snow.

SCREE: the product of the freeze-and-thaw erosion of cliffs lying at the angle of repose on the less steep slopes below their base.

SÉRAC (*French*): a block or pinnacle of ice in an ice-fall.

SHERPAS: Nepalese hillmen of Tibetan stock.

SKINS: fixed to the soles of skis with the hair lying towards the rear they allow the ski mountaineer to thrust his foot forward and upward but prevent a backward slide.

SKYHOOK: a small hook which can be used instead of a piton in extreme situations where there is no crack to take the latter.

SLAB: a smooth non-vertical leaf of rock. A vertical slab becomes a step or a wall.

SNAP LINK: a karabiner.

SNOW BLINDNESS: a painful condition of the eyes due to an excess of ultra-violet light.

SNOW BRIDGE: the lid of snow over a crevasse by which the mountaineer hopes to cross, stronger in the cold of early morning than later in the day when the sun has come to bear.

SOUNDING RODS: rods which screw together in sections used by rescue teams to search the debris of an avalanche for victims.

SPUR: a secondary ridge.

STANCE: a halting spot generally with a belay handy.

STEP: a sudden steepening of a ridge, glacier or mountain slope.

STIRRUPS: or étriers, clipped into a piton with the aid of a karabiner they transfer the climbers weight from his waist to his feet; often replaced nowadays by nylon tape slings.

TIGER: a first-class climber with a seemingly unquenchable thirst for high standard routes; the term is probably derived from the proficiency badge awarded by the Himalayan Club to Sherpas.

TRAVERSE: to cross a slope or cliff horizontally or (ascending/descending traverse) diagonally.

VERGLAS: hard, transparent ice on rock generally caused by freezing rain.

VIBRAMS: hard rubber-soled boots designed originally for Alpine conditions.

WEDGE: either metal or wood, can be jammed into a crack too wide to take a piton.

…owledgements

Mountaineering has long been imbued with a tradition of helpfulness – you look after the other man on the rope just as you know he will look after you. I had, however, no right to expect that the same spirit would extend to the compilation of this anthology which is, after all, no more than an activity on the periphery of the sport. But it did. I could not have wished for a greater degree of assistance than in fact I received.

I am particularly grateful to the contributors who not only produced their copy at relatively short notice but who also assisted me greatly in building up the collection of nearly twelve hundred pictures from which the final selection was eventually made. A special word of thanks is due to those kind enthusiasts who, having seen the plan of the book, had suggestions to make as to contents and sources of material. The State Tourist Departments in London of the Austrian, German, French, Italian and Swiss Governments allowed me to search through their photographic libraries and I am grateful to them for their courtesy and help.

I wish to thank the Alpine Club and the Mount Everest Foundation: the former for the use of their unique library and the latter for a number of photographs and for great help in checking names, heights and dates.

Mrs Longland, Assistant Secretary of the Alpine Club, helped me on numerous occasions and Mrs Jill Hinde typed the manuscript with speed and accuracy. I am most grateful to them and to Miss Joy Fisher of Arthur Barker Ltd who afforded me invaluable help and co-operation at all stages of the project.

I wish to join the Publishers in thanking Mr G. E. Green, Editor of Mountaineering for permission to use substantial portions of Lord Hunt's article 'British Youth in the Mountains' which originally appeared in the Spring 1967 issue of the British Mountaineering Council Journal and to the following for permission to reproduce their photographs in this book:

John Cleare for the photographs on pages 2 and 3, 119, 121, 216, 222, 261 and 291; *The Mount Everest Foundation* for the photographs on pages 10, 12, 13, 14, 15, 16, 19, 20, 21, 28 and 29, and 33; *Maynard Miller* for the photograph on page 22; *Norman Dyhrenfurth* for the photograph on page 23; *Barry Bishop* for the photograph on page 26; *James Whittaker* for the photograph on page 27; *Willi Unsoeld* for the photographs on pages 30 and 102; *Dr Tom Hornbein* for the photograph on page 31; *J. Brown and the British Baltoro Expedition 1956* for the photographs on pages 34 and 38; *L. G. McNaught-Davis and the British Baltoro Expedition 1956* for the photograph on page 37; *J. M. Hartog and the British Baltoro Expedition 1956* for the photographs on pages 36, 39, 40, 41, 97, 98 and 99, and 100; *Christian Bonington* for the photographs on pages 32, 47, 48, 49 (left), 52, 53, 54, 55 (top and bottom), 103 (left and right), 104 and 105, 110, 111, 114 (top and bottom), 115, 129 (top left), 164, 208, 213, 220 and 221, 228 (right), and 270; *The Swiss National Tourist Office* for the photographs on pages 43, 162, 230, 232, 234, 235, 238, 248, 249, 296 and 297; *Ian Clough* for the photographs on pages 44, 45, 48 and 124; *The Weekend Telegraph and Christian Bonington* for the photographs on pages 35, 46, 49 and 50; *John Amatt* for the photographs on pages 56, 57, 58, 59, 60, 61, 62, 63, 64, 65, 66, 67, 68, 69, 128, 133 and 277; *Michael Ward* for the photographs on pages 36, 71, 74, 75, 76 and 77; *Colin Fraser* for the photograph on page 78; *André Roche* for the photographs on pages 79, 80, 81, 82, 83, 250, 251, 253, 255, 256 and 257; *G. Sainsbury* for the photograph on page 84; *The Mountain Rescue Association of North America* for permission to use their insignia on page 85; *Ralph Uber and the Mountain Rescue Association of North America* for the photographs on pages 86 and 87; *The U.S. Air Force and the Mountain Rescue Association of North America* for the photographs taken from the helicopter and reproduced on pages 86 and 87; *C. S. Houston* for the photographs on pages 17, 91, 93, 95, 242 and 243; *G. B. Spenceley* for the photographs on pages 107, 109, 134 and 135; *Hamish MacInnes* for the photographs on pages 122, 126 and 127; *Ken Wilson* for the photographs on pages 118 and 120; *Richard Cook* for the photograph on page 123; *W. D. Brooker* for the photographs on pages 125 and 129; *Graham Tiso* for the photograph on page 129 (bottom); *Douglas Scott* for the photograph on page 130; *J. Stenhouse* for the photograph on page 131 (top); *David Bathgate* for the photograph at the bottom of page 131; *Brian Robertson* for the photograph on page 132; *Royal Robbins* for the photographs on pages 136, 137, 146 and 151; *Harry L. Daley* for the photographs on pages 138 and 139, 141, 148, 150, 152 and 153; *Glen Denny* for the photographs on pages 140, 142, 143, 224 and 225, 226, 227 and 293; *Joe Fitscher* for the photograph at the bottom of page 143; *Tom Frost* for the photographs on pages 144, 145, 147, 149, 228 and 229; *A. H. Griffin* for the photographs on pages 154 and 158; *C. Douglas Milner* for the photographs on pages 116, 117, 156 and 157, 159, 160, 161 and 163; *F. R. Brooke* for the photographs on pages 167, 169 (top), 170 and 171, 173, 174, 175, 176, 177 and 178, 294 and 295; *Bradford Washburn* for the photographs on pages 182 and 183, 184 and 185, 188 and 189; *Michael Westmacott* for the photographs on pages 181, 186 and 187; *H. W. Tilman* for the photographs on pages 169 (bottom), 172, 190, 191, 195 and 196; *G. J. Pert* for the photographs on pages 192 and 193, and 194; *Firmin Photographs Ltd* for the photographs on pages 198, 199, 200 and 201; *Alfred Gregory* for the photographs on pages 202 and 203; *E. E. Shipton* for the photographs on pages 205, 206, 207, 209, 210, 211, 213, 214 and 215, 216, 217, 218, 219, 278 and 279; *The Canadian Government Travel Bureau* for the photographs on pages 236 and 237, and 239; *The Italian State Tourist Office* for the photograph on pages 246 and 247; *The New Zealand High Commission* for the photograph on page 263; *John Jackson* for the photographs on pages 269, 271, 272 and 273, 286 and 287; *Tom Weir* for the photograph on page 275; *The German National Tourist Office* for the photographs on pages 282 and 285; *N. E. Odell* for the photograph on page 289; *Rennie Bere* for the photograph on page 244; *Monica Jackson* for the photographs on pages 259, 264, 265, 267 and 280; and *Sir Douglas Busk* for the photograph on page 241.